Organically Raised

Organically Raised

Conscious Cooking for Babies and Toddlers

Anni Daulter

with Shanté Lanay

photography by Gina Sabatella

RODALE

This book is intended as a reference volume only, not as a medical manual. The information given here is designed to help you make informed decisions about your health. It is not intended as a substitute for any treatment that may have been prescribed by your doctor. If you suspect that you have a medical problem, we urge you to seek competent medical help.

Mention of specific companies, organizations, or authorities in this book does not imply endorsement by the author or publisher, nor does mention of specific companies, organizations, or authorities imply that they endorse this book, its author, or the publisher.

Internet addresses and telephone numbers given in this book were accurate at the time it went to press.

Rodale books may be purchased for business or promotional use or for special sales. For information, please write to:

Special Markets Department, Rodale Inc., 733 Third Avenue, New York, NY 10017

Printed in the United States of America

Rodale Inc. makes every effort to use acid-free ⊖, recycled paper ♻.

Book design by Christina Gaugler

Library of Congress Cataloging-in-Publication Data
Daulter, Anni.
    Organically raised : conscious cooking for babies and toddlers / by Anni Daulter with Shanté Lanay.
        p.   cm.
    Includes bibliographical references and index.
    ISBN-13 978–1–60529–643–2 pbk.
    ISBN-10 1–60529–643–0 pbk.
  1. Cookery (Baby foods)   2. Cookery (Natural foods)   3. Infants—Nutrition.   I. Lanay, Shanté.   II. Title.
    TX740.D335 2010
    641.5'622—dc22   2010005135

Distributed to the trade by Macmillan

2 4 6 8 10 9 7 5 3 1   paperback

RODALE
LIVE YOUR WHOLE LIFE™

We inspire and enable people to improve their lives and the world around them
For more of our products visit **rodalestore.com** or call 800-848-4735

*This book is dedicated to my amazing family. My loving husband, Tim; my artistic
and culinary adventuring son, Zoë; my fairy princess daughter, Lotus Sunshine; my sweet
and silly baby boy, Bodhi Ocean; and my newest little addition growing inside. You all mean
the world to me. With your love and support, I have been able to realize this dream.
I love you all more than all the love ever mixed into any recipe ever made!*

*In gratitude,
Mama Anni*

*This book is also dedicated to all the babies and little ones who will feed
and feast on these recipes as they grow throughout their lives.*

*For Mackenzie, my free-spirited, beautiful daughter: You have shown me
the true meaning of love. My greatest joy comes from the twinkle in your eyes!
I look forward to growing with you and watching you blossom.*

*For RJ and Rian, the world's two most compassionate brothers and uncles. My Dad, the most loving
man I have ever known. And finally, for my dearest mother: With every crazy idea and lifestyle
change, you have continuously supported and inspired me. I love you all more than words can express.*

*Peace and Blessings,
Shanté*

Contents

PART ONE
Awakening

PART TWO
Enlightenment

My Story

Twelve years ago, when my first son, Zoë, was a baby, I realized that the options for baby food were limited and their only appeal was their convenience. I was determined to make all of my son's food from scratch using ingredients from the local farmers' market. The problem was, I did not know how to cook! I slowly taught myself the ins and outs of baby-food making, did research on nutrition, experimented with many successful and not-so-successful recipes, and subsequently learned a lot about the joys and challenges of cooking for babies. What I realized through it all was that as a mom, I really did want the absolute best for my baby, and I was willing to do whatever it took to make that happen. I knew that other parents felt the way I did, especially in regard to nutrition and food. Thus, with the birth of my second child, Lotus, my own baby food company—Bohemian Baby Fresh Organic Baby Food—was also born. I began by writing down some of my children's favor-

ite recipes and feeding all the babies I knew. Bohemian Baby was created out of my desire to help busy parents feed their babies the best possible foods in the most convenient way. I wanted to make foods that were fresh, organic, and reflective of different cultural cuisines. Most important, I wanted to produce foods that tasted great! When I saw that babies were falling in love with my food, I knew I was onto something.

As my passion for food grew, so did my understanding of how important it is to respect and honor the art of cooking, even when the meal might consist of only a single-ingredient puree. Before I became a mother, Buddhist monks taught me that "conscious cooking" is the art of preparing meals with awareness and presence, which infuses the food with higher energy. This spiritual education taught me how to pour love into every recipe and bring my mind to a calm awareness when I cook so that I always remember to care for and appreciate those around me. Food can nurture more than your body; when prepared with positive intentions, it can feed the soul. Recently, I've used the lessons and insights I've gained from these experiences to develop even more helpful tools for parents on my Conscious Family Living Web site. Please visit me regularly to learn all kinds of natural parenting tips at www. consciousfamilyliving.com.

I have fed a lot of babies over the past few years. I am always touched by the enormous responsibility that comes with feeding a brand-new baby. A newborn has an untouched system, and I would never feed another parent's baby anything I would not feed my own child. The hours spent discussing special diets, likes and dislikes, and eating frustrations with parents have allowed me to get to know dozens of babies. Many of the recipes in *Organically Raised* are named after the babies and toddlers who inspired them. All of the recipes in this book have been developed from the heart. I hope you and your little ones find them delectable. It is an honor to have a chance to feed your baby. Together, we can make kids healthier and happier!

In gratitude,

Anni

Foreword

You're in for a treat! Anni's delicious recipes and her approach to conscious cooking will help your family celebrate many wonderful meals together. Few things in life are more important than this.

Our children are built from food. When we look in their eyes or smile at their smiles or kiss their skinned knees, those eyes, teeth, and joints were built from food. This alone should make us pause and choose to give our children the very best to eat.

Food does more than strengthen our children's bodies . . . it also fuels their journeys through the world. It is the energy behind each step, each hug, each discovery, and each mood. Even our consciousness, and each new insight learned, is linked to food. The connections in our brains are built from food; our memories are built from food. And when we share food with our children, we share life.

Many people are dismayed about how the typical American school-aged child eats today, and I share their concern. Most of the major children's health problems on the increase today—including ADHD, allergies, asthma, diabetes, eczema, learning disabilities, obesity, and some childhood cancers—can be linked to today's diet: either too little of the great things children should be getting from food, or too much of what they shouldn't.

But food habits start much earlier. How our children eat as babies and toddlers sets the stage for the food and quantity preferences that can influence them for the rest of their lives. What a delicious opportunity!

In my book *Feeding Baby Green,* I help parents learn how to train their children's palates without fuss and without battle. I give parents what they need to teach "Nutritional Intelligence: the age-appropriate ability to recognize and enjoy healthy amounts of great food.

Anni takes this concept home. She gives you what you need to learn—*Cooking Intelligence*: the conscious, joyful ability to prepare healthy amounts of great food for your family. This ancient skill, passed down from generation to generation, has been all but lost in recent years.

Her recipes have evolved over time after being tested by hundreds of babies. You can trust that the food you make from this book will be both nutritionally sound and delicious. Whether you've never cooked much before or you cook every day, let Anni guide you on a delectable journey of love and creation that will nourish your child inside and out.

Alan Greene, MD, FAAP
Professor of Pediatrics, Stanford University School of Medicine;
Author, Raising Baby Green *and* Feeding Baby Green;
Co-creator, DrGreene.com

Introduction

Cooking Awareness: A Guide to Conscious Cooking

Many parents don't understand the basics of healthy eating and how the rules of nutrition apply to babies and toddlers. So much information on well-rounded diets is available today that it can be daunting to decide what to feed your children. But I can help you. When it comes to preparing meals for babies and toddlers, I use a simple philosophy that I call the Fundamental Five:

organic • mindful • seasonal • flavorful • international

THE FUNDAMENTAL FIVE

Organic

Organic food is raised without the use of pesticides or synthetic fertilizers. Organic foods limit your children's exposure to agricultural chemicals. Keeping chemicals out of our food supply, our soil, and our water is simply healthier for our children, ourselves, and our planet.

Mindful

How we prepare food is as important as the food itself. When we cook with loving intentions, it enhances the flavor and overall experience of the meal for everyone. Babies' and toddlers' first bites of foods and flavors are sacred introductions to nutritional habits and tastes that will last a lifetime. If you follow the Fundamental Five philosophy when you cook, all the meals you prepare for your children will be fresh, nutritious, and tasty.

Seasonal

All fruits and vegetables peak at different seasons of the year. By providing your children with foods that are in season, you can offer them a diversity of fresh, tasty flavors. Our bodies need different nutrients at different times of the year; when you eat with the seasons, your body is in rhythm with nature and operates in the best of health. Seasonal food is often more affordable, too.

Flavorful

When you offer foods that taste appetizing to young children, there is no need to resort to airplane games and bribes. Babies—just like adults—really do care about taste.

International

All over the world, babies and toddlers eat their local cuisine—food that often includes a wide variety of spices and flavors. Unfortunately, most babies in the United States do not try flavors from other cultures. If you introduce your babies to international flavors, you will expand their culinary palates and get them excited about eating diverse foods.

MORE ABOUT ORGANIC FOOD

Our babies arrive in this world with pure, untouched bodies. As we begin to feed them solid foods, their bodies use the nutrients to grow rapidly. Most new parents have heard of organic food but may not understand its true importance, especially for babies.

The chemicals used in conventional farming leave a residue on the produce. These toxins can build up in our bodies and cause health issues. In fact, the Organic Consumers Association reports that chemical pesticides are now found in the blood of 95 percent of Americans, and the levels are twice as high in children as in adults. Exposure to chemical pesticides has been linked to incidence of hyperactivity, behavior disorders, learning disabilities, developmental delays, and motor dysfunction in children. Food is one of the main sources of pesticide exposure for children in the United States.

By feeding your baby organic food, you are choosing to nourish him with toxin-free

food and to protect him from potential disease. The long-term effects from eating pesticide-sprayed food aren't known yet, but there is no need to take chances with your baby's health when organic products are widely available.

Incorporating organic eating into your lifestyle may demand more thought, time, commitment, and active participation, but your efforts will reward your baby with more taste, vitality, and well-being.

ORGANIC SHOPPING TIPS

Changing your eating habits can be an exciting adventure. You don't have to make this change all at once. If you ease into these new habits, it will lead to long-lasting results. Here are some tips that can help you make the adjustment.

Start Simple

Begin by purchasing fewer packaged, shelf-stable foods. In general, these are more expensive, excessively processed, and less nutritious than food you prepare at home.

Keep an Eye on Expense

Organic foods used to be significantly more expensive than conventional foods, but many major chain supermarkets are branding their own lines of organic products at competitive prices. At times it may be hard to shop all organic, so just do your best. Start by purchasing organic versions of dairy products like milk, cheese, and eggs, as well as fruits grown directly on the ground, and root vegetables, as these foods are the most likely to have been hit with hormones or pesticides. The Web site www.foodnews.org provides a list of high- and low-sprayed produce. Or consider utilizing your green thumb and growing organic produce yourself—gardening with children can be fun and rewarding. You can also reduce your organic grocery bill by participating in a food co-op or shopping locally at the farmers' market.

Read Labels

Don't be fooled! "Conventionally grown" does not mean "organic." When produce is labeled as "conventionally grown," that means the farmers may have used pesticides and other synthetic chemicals to grow the food. Look for "certified organic" symbols when buying your produce. Just because food is sold in health food stores does not make it healthy.

Shop Locally

By purchasing locally grown foods at your community farmers' market, you learn to be conscious of where and how your food is grown and become acquainted with the seasonal foods available in your area. Supporting local farmers benefits your local economy, the environment, and your family's eating habits. Taking your children to the farmers' market teaches them how to identify and select fresh foods. If you do not have access to a farmers' market, look for a local pick-your-own farm. These farms exist all over the country; they allow you and your family to pick fruits and vegetables right off the tree or plant. When you type in your zip code, Local Harvest (http://www.localharvest.org) shows you the nearest farmer's market.

Set a Good Example

Eating organic foods should be a priority for you as well as your children. If our children see us paying attention to what we eat, there's a better chance that they will do the same. We all need to help preserve our planet by incorporating eco-consciousness into our everyday lives, including how we nourish our bodies. So let's all eat organic!

PART ONE

Awakening

CHAPTER 1

Getting Started

WELCOME TO THE WORLD, BRAND-NEW BABY

New parents are overloaded with so much information and so many opinions that it is easy to get overwhelmed. But here is my simple advice to new moms and dads: Always listen to your instincts first. Pay close attention to your baby's needs and the different ways he communicates with you. This will help you in all aspects of parenting!

As your baby begins to eat, he experiences a culinary awakening that is truly magnificent. A newborn is the ultimate tabula rasa, or blank slate, and he is depending on you to guide him to his culinary destiny.

I encourage you, as a new parent, to awaken your own senses and curiosities around food. I hope that the ideas in this book will intrigue you, encourage you to try new ways of cooking, and expand the food vocabulary of your entire family.

SACRED MAMA'S MILK

Women's bodies are designed to feed babies. Mama's milk is nature's best all-around organic superfood: It has just the right amount of fat, sugar, water, and protein to help her baby grow and develop. Breast milk is rich in natural antibodies that help newborns fight off bacteria and viruses. Studies show that breastfed babies have improved brain growth and development, better vision, and strengthened immune systems, which leads to fewer chronic illnesses.[1]

Not only is nursing the most nutritious beginning for your baby, but it is also convenient and cost effective. Breast milk is always the right temperature. There are no financial costs involved, no need to measure out formula or scrub bottles. When you choose to breastfeed your baby, you are committing the time to get to know her intimately. The sacred practice of breastfeeding helps you bond with your new baby.

And here's a nursing bonus: Mamas can burn up to 800 calories per day while breast-feeding, which can help shed those extra pounds gained during pregnancy!

Breastfeeding and Weaning

The American Academy of Pediatrics currently recommends breastfeeding for a minimum of 1 year—longer, if desired.

The average age worldwide for weaning a baby from breast milk is between years 5 and 7. Mothers around the world choose to wean at different times; breastfeed your baby as long as both of you feel comfortable. If you allow the rhythm of nursing to unfold naturally, the weaning process will occur seamlessly. Trust me, your baby will not want breast milk forever, even though you may think so at times!

Feeding Schedules

Generally, if your baby is thriving and has no specific medical concerns, you do not need to wake him up to eat. Most newborns will want to be fed every 2-3 hours, but some may require feeding every hour. If you have concerns about how much breastmilk your baby is getting, it is a good idea to consult your local lactation expert and/or pediatrician. Babies will always let you know when they are hungry, and it is best to follow their body rhythms rather than impose your own schedule. Trust your baby, and learn the unique language between the two of you.

As your baby grows, he will usually adjust his feeding schedule on his own. Remember that even though babies can start eating solids around 6 months, which is also the American Academy of Pediatrics'

Nursing Tip

The La Leche League is a nonprofit organization that offers support and advice for nursing mothers. Should you have questions or need support during your time nursing, please seek their guidance. The mamas in La Leche League possess both wisdom and strength. I highly recommend their skills and services.

recommendation, first foods should be a supplement to mama's milk or formula. The primary source of nutrition for your baby up to age 1 should be breast milk.

Formula and Feeding When You're Away

While I advocate breastfeeding on cue, that practice is not possible in every situation. When you can't breastfeed your baby directly, you may want to try expressing your milk with a pump so that your baby still has the opportunity to get the best nutrition possible even while you are away. If that is not possible, then turn to one of a number of organic baby formulas on the market today. Make sure the brand you choose is DHA-enriched, and full of decosahexaenoic acid which helps with brain development and makes formula closer to breast milk.

Be mindful of your choice of bottles. Some plastic bottles, when heated give off a chemical called bisphenol A, BPA, which can be toxic to babies and young children. There are some BPA free companies like Born Free, that make safe plastic bottles for babies, or you may consider glass bottles. Environmental health reports have recommended using glass bottles as a result.[2] Dr. Brown's and Evenflo both make cost-effective glass bottles, and new companies are creating glass bottles with safety sleeves that guard against breakage.

Milk and Milk Alternatives

You may start introducing soy milk or cow's milk to your baby's diet starting at age 1, although your infant will not need it if you continue to breastfeed often.

Currently, there is a debate about the health benefits of cow's milk. The proteins in cow's milk differ from those found in human milk and may cause problems of digestion and intolerance, impair the absorption of nutrients, and cause autoimmune reactions. Bovine milk fat does not have the necessary saturated fats and cholesterol found in human mother's milk.

Many cows are injected with genetically engineered hormones, such as Bovine Growth Hormone, to increase their milk production.[3] Due to their high dietary food and water requirements, cows often ingest significant levels of pesticides and pollutants, which are then concentrated in their milk fat. The amount of drugs now given to cows adds to this chemical soup.[4] The concern over the purity of cow's milk has led more folks to buy organic milk with no hormones present or to purchase milk alternatives, such as goat's milk. Be sure to read labels, as even alternative milk may contain additives, or may not contain adequate vitamin D or calcium.

CHAPTER 2

Conscious Kitchen

THE FIRST INGREDIENT: MINDFULNESS

When you enter your kitchen ready to prepare a meal, you more than likely think about *what* you are going to prepare rather than focus on *how* you will make it. You probably check to see if you have all of the ingredients for your dish, then you get out your recipe and gather the necessary cookware. These steps are only the beginning of creating great meals: Delicious foods are made with our creative vision, our physical hands, and mostly with our passion, pure and simple! Truly remarkable food starts with fresh ingredients and a fresh perspective from you.

Mindfulness is the essence of "conscious cooking." It encourages us as parents to deepen our understanding of our own relationship with food and helps us be more conscious about nutritional traditions we wish to pass along to our families. When you start cooking with a sense of the sacred in mind, you begin to see how your love for everything wells up in your heart. When you cook like this, every stew is special and every grain of rice a miracle. In my home, one thing we do is hold family cooking days. My husband and I and all the kids take turns choosing the menu. Then we all spend the day preparing it, from buying or picking the ingredients, assembling and cooking the meal, setting the table or outside picnic blanket, and finally enjoying a wonderful family meal together. This practice keeps us all connected, communicating, laughing, and enjoying the food that we made with our love for each other.

What does it mean to be mindful? It means not worrying about later and focusing on the "now"—living in the moment. When you focus on the culinary task at hand rather than fret about paying bills, for example, you give an added boost of love to the meal you are making. Being focused when we prepare foods, making conscious decisions to eat family meals together, and infusing our food preparations with our happy intentions—these are the foundation of mindfulness. This practice can truly strengthen relationships and bring families closer together.

mindful tip

Be aware of your mood as you begin your cooking process. Let stress melt away by taking three deep breaths, each time inhaling love and exhaling stress. Allow the joy of cooking for your family to fill your body and mind.

Nothing inspires me more than thinking about how much I love my children and how much I want to provide them with the best possible life. Focusing on these thoughts allows me to shift my energy so that I begin cooking with a high level of positive consciousness. I become acutely aware of my surroundings and absorbed in every action in the kitchen, from washing my hands to cleaning and cutting the vegetables. I visualize my love for my family coming through my hands as I prepare each sacred meal. Consider that what you are making will satisfy and strengthen them. This is a meditation of sorts, a way of extending your love for your family that will leave you feeling good inside even as you create delicious, healthy foods. Try reciting the following Mama Mantra during the preparation:

MAMA MANTRA

"I wish to nourish your growing body and gentle spirit with every bite and to give you the best fresh foods I can."

SACRED SPACE

The most crucial ingredient in your kitchen isn't a piece of equipment, a spice, or even a stove. Creating a truly "conscious kitchen" means making your space your own and infusing it with your good intentions when you cook for your loved ones. Even if you do not have a lot of room, try to keep your cooking area clean and uncluttered. Make a comfortable environment for yourself by lighting candles, playing your favorite music, or doing anything else that calms and inspires you. Remind yourself to relax, breathe, and be in the moment; this is the essence of *conscious cooking*. It can help you appreciate your life with your family more deeply.

Here are some tips to help you cook consciously when you are starting to prepare meals for your family.

1. Smile! The simple act of smiling can brighten your mood and lift your spirits.

2. Decorate your cooking space with photos of your family. The pictures will remind you why you're preparing each meal.

3. Find a way to mark the beginning and end of your meal preparation. For example, ring a small gong or put on some relaxing music.

4. Hang this mantra in your kitchen: "Every meal prepared in this kitchen will be done with love, joy, and the intention of feeding my family in body, mind, and spirit."

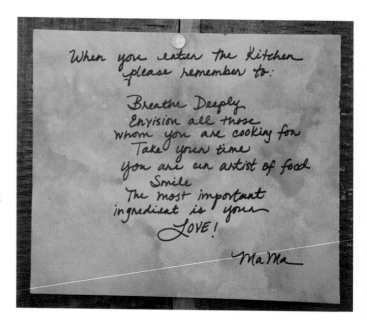

EQUIPMENT

You need only a few basic items to prepare baby and toddler food, and you may have most of them in your kitchen already.

Steamer

You will use a steamer frequently. If you don't own this tool, purchasing one will be a worthwhile investment. Select one with both deep and shallow baskets to steam different sizes of fruits and veggies.

Food Processor

It is essential that you invest in either a food processor or a blender to puree your baby's food. These appliances come in various sizes, and any type will work. A medium-size food processor will allow you to puree enough food for a few meals at a time.

Food Mills

Handheld and electric food mills are convenient on the go or to use at home to prepare a small batch of baby food. Environmentally friendly, or "green," food mills are available now.

As a bonus, you can use a food mill for chopping herbs and spices, which saves you the chore of cleaning out the food processor.

Coffee Grinder

Dedicate one coffee grinder exclusively to food preparation. It will come in handy when you are grinding whole grains to a powder to make cereals.

Glass Jars

Use glass jars to store baby and toddler foods. Unlike plastic containers, glass won't affect the flavor of the food. Buy canning jars in the supermarket, or pick up a collection of small glass jars at your local Cost Plus World Market or Pier 1 Imports. You can even use small glass bowls with airtight lids, or re-use baby food jars you have around the house. Try freecycle.org for glass jars, too. A nice "green" idea!

Glass Baking Dishes

These are ideal for baking vegetables like butternut squash, pumpkin, and sweet potato.

Rubber Spatulas

Rubber spatulas get all of the puree mixtures out of the food processor and into your jars.

Label Maker

This allows you to note the contents of the jars as well as the date of preparation. Try freecycle.org to find unused labels.

Dishes, Utensils, and More

Minimize the use of plastic by using real glass or ceramic plates, bowls, cups, and utensils for your children. Many plastic products contain BPA (bisphenol A), which can leach hazardous toxins into food. For babies who are not quite ready for glass or ceramic, consider using wooden or stainless steel containers.

Sippy Cups

Stainless steel sippy cups are available from Klean Kanteen and Safe Sippy, so you don't have to rely on plastic. Born Free plastic bottles and sippy cups are BPA free and safe to use. You

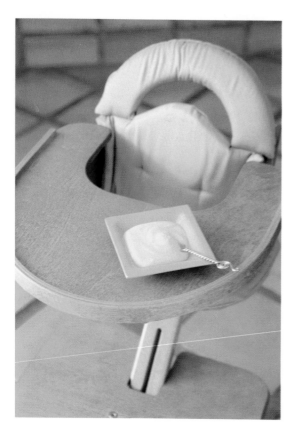

may, however, choose not to use sippy cups at all: You could have your baby drink from a regular cup after age 1. With patience on your part, your baby will learn how to use the open-top cup without spilling.

Extra Equipment

Beaba Babycook is a compact countertop appliance that multitasks as a food steamer, blender, warmer, and defroster. It's also great for preparing the mix-ins for toddler and preschooler foods (see Chapter 8).

Tables and Chairs

It is important for your baby to feel like a part of your family right from the beginning, so let him eat with you at the table. Set a wooden high chair close by, or use one without a tray so it can be pushed right up to the table.

If your baby is a particularly messy eater (my son Bodhi certainly was!) and does not like to wear a bib, keep a few of his old shirts on hand. Store them in the kitchen with your dishtowels, pull one out for mealtime, and then simply toss it in the wash after the meal. Or let your baby eat without a shirt if that makes cleanup easier. Use a splat mat under the high chair to catch any falling or flying food that may leave your baby's spoon in moments of uncontrollable culinary excitement!

STORAGE AND REHEATING TECHNIQUES

Fresh Is Best

Most unopened homemade baby food keeps for 7 days in the refrigerator; it generally lasts about 3 to 4 days once unsealed. The idea of preparing your baby's food in bulk and freezing it in simple meal portions may sound appealing, but I urge you to resist this approach. When you freeze food, its molecular structure starts to break down, reducing the nutritional value and affecting the taste significantly. I often ask parents whether they prefer fresh or frozen green beans, and all of them respond: "Fresh!" I then ask them to imagine eating only frozen food. Yuck! The bottom line is that fresh is best, and if we are aiming for the best prepared foods for babies, then we should minimize frozen food when possible. That said, it is not always possible to make all of a baby's food from scratch, yet as a parent you still want healthy, fast options. My advice is to make fresh food as much as you

what to have on hand IN THE PANTRY

It's nice to be able to open the cupboard and have exactly what you need to prepare a meal. Here is a cheat sheet to make it simple.

WORLD FLAVORS AND SPICES	WHOLE GRAINS	HEALTHY GROUND MIX-INS
Balsamic vinegar	Barley	Açai berries
Basil	Millet	Chia seeds
bay leaves	Quinoa	Dried seaweed
Braggs amino acids (soy substitute)	Various pastas	Flaxseed
Cinnamon	Whole grain oats	Goji berries
Cumin		Wheat germ
Extra-virgin olive oil		
Garlic		
Mint		
Nutmeg		
Oregano		
Parsley		
Sesame oil		
Soy sauce		
Sunflower oil		
Thyme		
Turmeric		

can and freeze when you have to. Most important, you should not feel guilty if you can-not always prepare fresh foods. If you do choose to freeze some food, make sure that you use baby-safe BPA-free plastic containers, and never freeze glass. Frozen foods are best consumed within 4 to 6 weeks.

Avoid Microwave Heating

Reheating food by microwave oven is not much faster than by stove top, so why not take the extra seconds and follow the more natural approach? New studies have shown that microwaving food breaks down its nutritional content. To maintain food's purity and fresh taste, it's best to keep the elements we cook with as natural as possible.

CHAPTER 3

Hot Topics: Popular Mama Questions Answered

As a new mama (or papa), you're bound to have questions about food and feeding. In this chapter, we look at the most popular questions, beginning with the basics of feeding baby and then moving to discussions about vitamins, protein, fat, and other nutritional issues.

FEEDING BASICS

When Should My Baby Start Eating Solids?

Babies have delicate digestive systems and tiny tummies, which is why they need to eat small amounts many times throughout the day. Typically, pediatricians recommend that babies start tasting solids at around the age of 6 months or when they can sit up by themselves. When you are observing your baby's unique cues, you will see signs that she is ready to start her culinary journey. She may start grabbing at your food or show great interest in what you are putting in your mouth. Remember that your baby's first feedings are simply test-drives. Do not force a child to eat, and offer only one or two small spoonfuls at first.

What Are the Recommended First Foods?

In the past, the majority of pediatricians recommended rice cereal mixed with breast milk or formula as a first food. Today, many pediatricians advise parents to start with fresh pureed single-ingredient fruits and veggies—such as apples, pears, sweet potatoes, butternut squash, peas, avocados, or bananas. Rice cereal is bland and doesn't have much nutritional value, so why not start with something tasty? Whole grain cereals can be introduced around 7 months and should be mixed with a puree. You'll find several cereal recipes in Chapter 9.

How Much Should My Baby Eat at One Time?

Let your baby guide you. The quantity of food your baby eats will vary from day to day, sometimes by great amounts. Don't be surprised if one day she acts likes she's starving and the next day she eats like a bird. Simply offer your baby one spoonful at a time and go from there.

Choking Hazards

Avoid the following foods until your baby is older and you are confident he or she can chew well enough.

Dried fruit, raisins, cherries with pits, raw apple slices, pear slices, berries

Grapes (cut into quarters and given only after your baby is at least 1 year old)

Hard or chewy candy, gum, jelly beans

Hot dogs

Peanut butter

Popcorn, pretzels

Tree nuts (almonds, cashews, pecans, pistachios, macadamias, pine nuts, walnuts)

Vegetables like raw carrot sticks

What If My Baby Is Not Interested in Solid Foods at All?

During baby's first year, food is a supplement to breast milk or formula, not the primary source of nutrition. Don't rush to start solids; let your baby set the pace. First bites should be *little* bites. Some babies develop an interest in food earlier than others. In my experience, boys generally tend to eat more than girls in the beginning. There's no need to worry if your baby does not show an interest in food for several months; eventually, she will. And when she does try new foods, keep in mind that a baby may need to be introduced to a particular food up to 10 times before she will show an active interest in it. Your baby may make faces when you introduce solid foods, but that is primarily because she is not used to the sensations and textures. Give your baby a chance to get accustomed to new tastes slowly. You can encourage her to try a new food by taste testing it yourself, so she sees that mommy and daddy like it.

What If I Can't Get My Baby to Eat Vegetables?

Many babies are delighted with vibrantly colored, fresh, seasonable vegetables. With toddlers, I suggest presenting the food in a fun way. You can make a happy face with the veggies, serve them in a colorful bowl, and tell stories about a protagonist who is aided by eating your vegetable of choice. Another technique is to incorporate vegetables into foods your toddler already loves by using vegetable purees as pasta sauces or dips or adding bite-size veggies to favorite family meals. Remember that you are an example: If you regularly eat vegetables and enjoy them, your child will imitate you.

What about Juice?

Jay Gordon, MD, says, "Juices are another traditional food that almost every baby learns to love. They are mostly sugar and water because the best part of the apple or pear gets left behind."[1]

According to the American Academy of Pediatrics, juice offers no nutritional benefits over whole fruit. Intake of juice should be completely avoided for infants and limited to 4 to 6 ounces per day for children 1 to 6 years old. The AAP notes that many parents find juice boxes convenient; however, like soda, juice can contribute to energy imbalance.[2] Juice tricks the body into feeling like it's full and does not give children the opportunity to eat good foods. Alternatives to juice include plain water flavored with fresh fruit or cucumbers, juice diluted with water, and herbal teas.

Many parents don't think of offering tea to children, but herbal tea has no caffeine and offers many health benefits for everyone. Both chamomile and peppermint tea can soothe an upset tummy or calm down nerves, and children find them tasty. Herbal teas are a great alternative to sugar-filled juices. You can offer the tea with no added sweetener or—for a healthy alternative to sugar—with a little agave nectar.

> **MAMA WISDOM**
>
> "My daughter Mackenzie loves what we call fancy water. Some days it will be water and mint; other days she has slices of heart-shaped cucumbers in it. For further variety, we have days with fresh organic berries and fruits added to water."
>
> Shanté, mama to Mackenzie, age 3

VITAMIN TALK: IRON

Iron is good for the brain and strengthens the immune system. It is a component of hemo-globin (red blood cells), which carries oxygen throughout the body. The Recommended Dietary Allowance (RDA) of iron for babies 1 year or less is 6 to 10 milligrams per day. This increases to 10 milligrams per day from 1 to 3 years of age. Iron-fortified rice cereal, iron-fortified oatmeal, cooked beans, molasses, prunes, spinach, sweet potatoes, and peas are all good sources of iron.[3]

VITAMIN TALK: CALCIUM

Calcium is essential to the development of healthy bones, teeth, muscles, and nerves. The RDA for calcium in babies 1 year or less can be adequately covered by daily breast milk and/or formula feedings. The calcium requirement levels off at 500 milligrams per day for toddlers and 800 milligrams per day during the preschool years. This can be met by encouraging your child to drink 16 to 24 ounces of milk each day. Calcium is also found in nondairy sources such as broccoli, kale, hummus, fortified soy milk, and flaxseed, among others.[4]

PROTEIN

Protein is vital to nearly all the biological processes in the body. It also provides energy for your baby. Babies under the age of 1 need 1 gram of protein per pound of body weight per day. From 12 to 15 months, they need ½ gram of protein per pound of body weight. This is a much smaller amount than most of us assume we need. For example, a 3-year-old who weighs approximately 30 pounds needs only 16 grams (approximately ½ ounce) of protein a day. A grown adult weighing 130 pounds needs approximately 2½ ounces of protein a day.[5] Regardless of your family's diet preferences, there are abundant protein options to pick and choose from that will ensure your child achieves adequate protein intake.

Plant-Based Proteins

Simply by serving a wide variety of whole foods, you can rest assured your children will get the protein they need. Plant-based protein sources like legumes are high in fiber and contain healthy unsaturated fats, making them a powerhouse of protein and nutrition. I have found that black, kidney, and pinto beans are a huge hit with small children. Black-eyed peas, split peas, lentils, vegetarian baked beans, vegetarian refried beans, hummus, falafel, hemp, and grains such as oats, quinoa, and wheat are also high in protein. For children who are a little older and don't have a nut allergy, nut butters such as almond, cashew, and peanut can be served as healthy dips with veggies or spread on sandwiches. Most nuts offer healthy fats in addition to protein, and those good fats support brain development.

Organic soy milk is readily available in most grocery stores, and several companies offer soy milk boxes convenient for young children. For older children, edamame and soy nuts are good on-the-go snacks. There are also soy-based "meat" products like faux chicken nuggets, bacon, sausage, and hot dogs; meatless burgers; and meat substitutes such as tempeh and tofu. The US Food and Drug Administration considers soy to be complete protein and a good substitute for animal products.[6]

When shopping for plant-based proteins, I try to purchase locally at a farmers' market, food co-op, or health food store whenever possible. Take your child along, and encourage her to select and scoop out the color of lentil or type of dried bean she would like from the bulk bins. Kids love to help, and involving them in the process reduces meltdowns while shopping and encourages youngsters to eat the food once it's prepared. As with any type of food, plant-based proteins are not created equal. Be sure to read product labels to check for total fat and carbohydrate content.

Protein from Meat

Adding meat to your child's diet is a personal choice. Including small amounts of meat in her culinary repertoire after she is at least 12 months old is one way of contributing to her intake of complete proteins, which are vital to development. When shopping for meat, you should opt for items that are organically fed, free-range, cage free, and free of all antibiotics and hormones, including growth hormones.[7] National regulations set for certified organic farms require that farmers give animals only "organic feed" free of animal parts and allow the animals access to the outdoors, which reduces stress. To help minimize disease, organic farmers use preventive measures such as clean housing, rotational grazing, and a balanced diet.[8] When you shop for fish, opt for sustainable healthy choices: Wild fish is most often better than farm raised. Purchasing healthier cuts of meat may be more expensive, but the investment ensures your child gets the maximum benefits while keeping her small digestive system free of harmful substances. Since children need only small amounts of protein, remain mindful of the serving size of the meat.

> **DADDY WISDOM**
>
> *"As with most families, my children's diet reflects my own, which includes various types of lean meat. They especially like slow-cooked meat, which is easy to chew and served with some form of sauce. A favorite in our house is teriyaki chicken either served on skewers with rice and vegetables or included in a stir-fry."*
>
> Darryl, daddy to Leah,
> age 13, and Cy, age 5

Note: There is no such designation as USDA organic fish. Currently, fish labeled as organic is not from the United States and therefore not held to the same federal standards.[9]

Some children like meat more than others do. It's not uncommon for different family members to have separate food preferences. In my own family, I have one child who is a strict vegetarian, one who loves meat, and one who loves all types of food. As parents, we need to be sensitive to our children's preferences and serve the healthiest food available.

FAT

According to the FDA, a 2-year-old should not have more than 2 teaspoons of fat per day. Fat provides energy and contributes to your child's developing nervous sytem and brain function. It protects vital organs, provides insulation to keep your child warm, and helps with the absorption of fat-soluble vitamins. Unsaturated fats are the most healthy—you can find these in avocados, vegetable oils, wild fish, and seed and nut oils. Flaxseed and flaxseed oil contain a type of unsaturated fat called essential fatty acids. Chia seeds are also great.

They provide a boost of healthy fat to your baby. You should limit the amount of saturated fat your child receives and avoid hydrogenated fats, including trans fats.[10]

WHAT'S UP? EVERYTHING YOU WOULD ASK A NUTRITIONIST IF YOU COULD!

What's Up with Nitrates?

Nitrates are a chemical preservative that studies suggest are converted into cancer-causing agents and that may be linked to leukemia in children and to type 2 diabetes. Nitrates are most commonly found in the groundwater of fields that have been sprayed with pesticides—yet another reason to eat organic food. Root vegetables (such as carrots) and leafy vegetables (like spinach and kale) have been found to have especially high concentrations of nitrates.[11] Nitrates are also found in cured meats such as hot dogs, cold cuts, ham, bacon, and burgers.

American Academy of Pediatrics Statements on Nitrates

"Because the intake of naturally occurring nitrates from foods such as green beans, carrots, squash, spinach, and beets can be as high as or higher than that from well water, these foods should be avoided before 3 months of age. . . . Infants fed commercially prepared infant foods after 3 months of age generally are not at risk of nitrate poisoning, although the containers should be refrigerated after first use and discarded within 24 hours of opening."

—AAP Nitrate Statement

"Because vegetables, including green beans, carrots, squash, spinach, and beets, can have nitrate levels as high or higher than that of well water, infants should not eat these foods until after age 3 months."

—AAP Well Water Statement

What's Up with Antioxidants?

Antioxidants are known for their antiaging effects on the brain, but they also protect the brain from damage by free radicals. Free radicals are unstable molecules that occur naturally in your body. Free radicals want to be stablized, so they steal electrons from healthy cells, thus making those cells less healthy. Antioxidants basically serve as a defense for your body and combat damage caused by free radicals. Simply put, they help keep you strong, vital, and healthy.

What's Up with Honey?

Although it has several medicinal properties, honey is *not* safe for infants under age 1; ingesting it can lead to life-threatening infant botulism. Botulinum spores are found widely in soil, dust, and honey. When an infant swallows the spores, they can germinate in the baby's immature gastrointestinal tract and begin producing botulinum toxin. This has occurred even when the honey was used only to sweeten a pacifier.[12] Once a child reaches 12 months of age, honey is safe to ingest.

What's Up with Nuts?

Tree nuts are a choking hazard for infants and toddlers and should be avoided until after age 2. If your child is younger than 2 years old and does not have a history of allergies, you can consider grinding up nuts in your coffee grinder and adding them to food as a nutritional supplement. Almonds, cashews, pecans, pistachios, macadamias, pine nuts, and walnuts are all examples of tree nuts. Peanuts are actually a legume, not a tree nut. Some individuals have allergies to both peanuts and tree nuts. If your child is allergic to peanuts, it's best to have him tested for tree nut allergies as well. If his allergy is solely to peanuts, he should be able to enjoy the great taste and nutrional value of tree nuts.

CHAPTER 4

Starting Solids

As you begin to transition your baby to solid foods, keep food color and season in mind. A simple way to offer enough variety and nutritional balance is to make sure your baby is eating the rainbow! Give your baby fruits and veggies that range in color from white, yellow, and orange to purple, green, and brown.

SEASONAL

In today's fast-paced, convenience-oriented world, where summer peaches from South America are available in the United States in the frozen depths of winter, it's easy to forget to eat only what is in season in our corner of the world. Modern food processing and distribution make most foods available year-round, and grocery stores shelves look much the same in December as they do in July. But eating with the seasons energizes your body with essential nutrients that you need at different times throughout the year. Imagine a vegetable garden in the dead of winter, then imagine this same garden on a sunny summer day. How different things are during these two times of year! The changes in growing conditions from spring to summer or fall to winter balance the earth's resources. And when you eat local food in season, you have access to the most cost-effective, nutrient-dense, and flavorful products.

What does this mean for little ones? Your baby's diet should also fluctuate to reflect

rainbow eating

Red raspberries, orange carrots, yellow squash, green asparagus, blue blueberries, purple eggplant, brown mushrooms, black beans . . . yes, it is simply that easy to eat the rainbow!

According to David Heber in his book *What Color Is Your Diet?* "each colored fruit or vegetable provides a unique benefit to the diet, so you don't want to eat only fruits and vegetables of a single color [but, rather, many different colors]."[1]

The red group—which includes foods such as strawberries, raspberries, tomatoes, and red peppers—contains high amounts of vitamin C.

The orange group, high in vitamin A, includes winter squash, sweet potatoes, pumpkin, cantaloupe, and carrots.

The green group's primary purpose is to provide energy to the body. Many green foods contain lutein (a phytochemical important for eye health) and folate (a water-soluble B vitamin). Green foods include kiwifruit, broccoli, asparagus, kale, and spinach.

The blue-to-purple group includes blueberries, blackberries, Concord grapes, and eggplant, which are all high in antioxidants called anthocyanin pigments. Antioxidants allow us to stay active longer and keep our memory and functioning intact as we age.[2]

By feeding your baby foods in a rainbow of colors, you ensure that he will have a diet with diverse tastes, textures, and nutrients. It is also a wonderful way to teach him about colors!

seasonal and regional variety. In different parts of the world, and even in different regions of a country, menus vary. Foods are less expensive when they are locally abundant and available from nearby farms or, better yet, a home garden.

I grow veggies in raised planting beds that my friend Conor built. (His fabulous business creates the MinifarmBox that folks use to make their own sustainable gardens.) One advantage of raised beds, says Conor, is that they produce up to twice the crop yield of conventional ground planting. They are easier to manage because you have greater control over the soil and the growing environment, and they are a lot easier on your back! With raised beds is that you do not need to have a huge yard to grow some of your own food—even people who live in apartments can have a MinifarmBox.

Small farmers are connected to the land they work. Many grow and supply different varieties and cultivars of fruits and vegetables through each season. These small farms rotate their crops frequently, a practice that replenishes the soil with nutrients and results in more nutrient-dense foods.

By adding seasonal foods to your menu, you ensure that your family is getting essential vitamins and minerals, including important antioxidants that protect the body from disease. Eating healthy is always in season! Be creative throughout the year. Let the natural foods of spring, summer, fall, and winter be your guide.

SEASONAL PRODUCE GUIDE

SPRING	SUMMER	FALL	WINTER	YEAR-ROUND
Apricots	Beets	Acorn squash	Belgian endive	Avocados
Artichokes	Bell peppers	Apples	Broccoli	Bananas
Asparagus	Blackberries	Belgian endive	Brussels sprouts	Bok choy
Butter lettuce	Blueberries	Butternut squash	Chestnuts	Broccolini
English peas	Boysenberries	Cauliflower	Dates	Cabbage
Honeydew melons	Cherries	Celery root	Grapefruit	Carrots
Mustard greens	Corn	Cherimoya	Green beans	Celery
Oranges	Eggplant	Cranberries	Kale	Coconut
Pineapple	Figs	Garlic	Kiwifruit	Leeks
Ramps	Garlic	Ginger	Mushrooms	Lemons
Rhubarb	Grapefruit	Guava	Oranges	Lettuce
Snow peas	Green peas	Huckleberries	Pummelo	Onions
Sorrel	Mango	Jicama	Radicchio	Papayas
Spinach	Nectarines	Kumquats	Red currants	Potatoes
Spring baby lettuce	Okra	Leeks	Rutabagas	
Sugar snap peas	Peaches	Mushrooms	Sweet potatoes	
	Plums	Parsnips	Tangerines	
	Radishes	Passion fruit	Turnips	
	Raspberries	Pear	Winter squash	
	Strawberries	Persimmons		
	String beans	Pineapple		
	Summer squash	Pomegranate		
	Tomatillos	Pumpkin		
	Tomatoes	Quince		
	Watermelon	Rutabagas		
	Zucchini	Shallots		
		Turnips		

CHAPTER 5

Organic Baby Basics Recipes

6 to 9 Months

RAW FIRST MEALS

Raw meals do not require any cooking, are easy to travel with, and offer a tasty introduction to solids. Here are a few simple dishes that will be great first bites for your baby.

pure avocado puree (*summer*)

Nutrient-dense avocados are ideal to introduce once babies are old enough to eat table foods. Soft in texture and easily digestible, avocados' natural "packaging" makes them convenient for on-the-go meals.[1]

Cut 2 large avocados in half and remove the pits. Scoop the flesh into a bowl. Mash the avocado flesh until it achieves a smooth consistency.

> NUTRIENTS
> Dietary fiber
> Magnesium
> Potassium
> Vitamin E

pure island papaya puree (*summer*)

Cholesterol- and fat-free papayas are full of flavor and easy for a new eater to digest. A supersoft papaya can be pureed raw. (Partially ripe papayas will need to be cooked; follow the recipe for pear puree on page 34. Make the choice to puree or cook after you have seen how ripe your fruit is.) When you prepare papaya for your baby, make sure to scoop out the black seeds and use only the flesh. Strain every batch of papaya puree. Some hard-to-digest filaments often survive the pureeing process.

> NUTRIENTS
> Dietary fiber
> Folate
> Vitamin A
> Vitamin C

pure banana puree (*spring*)

Bananas are easy to take on the go: Pack a fork and a bowl, then just peel and mash the fruit. Bananas are gentle on a baby's new digestive system. When mashed, they also make an excellent natural sweetener for baking.

> NUTRIENTS
> Calcium
> Dietary fiber
> Magnesium
> Potassium
> Vitamin A
> Vitamin B, especially folate
> Vitamin C

STONE FRUITS

Most large stone fruits—such peaches, plums, apricots, and nectarines—require similar preparation and approximately the same steaming time: 6 to 8 minutes. These fruits tend to be extra juicy and sweet in late spring and summer and are sure to be a hit with any baby.

pure peach puree (summer)

There is nothing like biting into a ripe summer peach. The natural sweetness is truly a remarkable experience. Wait until the peak of the season to feed your baby peaches; you'll get the best of the bunch. Your baby will devour these!

NUTRIENTS

Iron

Potassium

Vitamin A

Vitamin C

2 pounds yellow sweet peaches (4 large peaches)

1. Wash and peel the peaches. Remove the pits. Cut the fruit into 1-inch pieces.

2. Steam the peach pieces for 6 to 8 minutes, or until soft (a sharp knife will pass easily through the pieces). Fruit that is not completely ripe will need to steam longer. Reserve the liquid from the steamer.

3. Transfer the steamed peach pieces to a food processor and puree until smooth. Add the reserved liquid (if necessary) in scant ⅛-cup increments until the puree reaches the desired consistency and smoothness.

NOTE: White peaches also work well in this recipe, but they tend to require more steaming than yellow peaches to reach the same consistency.

Steaming Tip

When you are preparing food for your baby in a steamer, put about 2 cups of water in the bottom of the pot, let the water reach a slow boil, add food items to your basket, and then put the basket into the steamer pot and leave it there just until the items are soft enough to puree. It's important not to oversteam, as that could break down the nutritional value of the food.

MORE STONE FRUITS IDEAS:
PREPARE THE SAME WAY AS PEACHES

pure apricot puree *(spring)*

Apricots are high in fiber and low in calories. Dried apricots are especially high in vitamin A and make a quick, yummy snack for children over age 2.

> **NUTRIENTS**
> Dietary fiber
> Iron
> Potassium
> Vitamin A
> Vitamin C

pure nectarine puree *(summer)*

Although they are similar to peaches, nectarines have a unique taste and a low gylcemic index, which means the natural sugars present will not cause your child to experience a sugar rush. Go nectarines!

> **NUTRIENTS**
> Dietary fiber
> Protein
> Vitamin A
> Vitamin C

pure plum puree *(summer)*

Plums are an excellent source of antioxidants. You can use any locally grown variety—just make sure the plums are organic and ripe.

> **NUTRIENTS**
> Dietary fiber
> Potassium
> Vitamin A
> Vitamin B_2
>   (riboflavin)
> Vitamin C

OTHER TREE FRUITS

You can find many irresistible treats hanging from the limbs of trees. Tree fruits have a silky, baby-friendly texture; their purees are wonderful for brand-new eaters. In fact, these basic purees are so healthy and flavorful that they're sure to become staples in your home.

pure pear puree *(fall)*

There is nothing like fresh pears. With their beautiful white color and gentle, sweet flavor, they make an excellent solid food for your baby.

2 pounds pears (4 large pears)

1. Wash and peel the pears. Core and cut into 1-inch pieces.

2. Steam the pear pieces for 8 to 10 minutes, or until soft (a sharp knife will pass easily through the pieces). Fruit that is not completely ripe will need to steam longer. Reserve the liquid from the steamer.

3. Transfer the steamed pear pieces to a food processor and puree until smooth. Add the reserved liquid (if necessary) in scant ⅛-cup increments until the puree reaches the desired consistency and smoothness.

Note: Extremely ripe pears will turn brown (oxidize) quickly. If you have overripe pears, get them over the steam as quickly as possible after peeling to minimize browning.

> **NUTRIENTS**
> Dietary fiber
> Potassium
> Vitamin A
> Vitamin C

> **MAMA MANTRA**
> *"I'm dedicated to feeding my baby healthy, nutritious first foods."*

MORE TREE FRUIT IDEAS: PREPARE THE SAME WAY AS PEARS

pure mango puree *(summer)*

Mangoes are delicious. Some have hairlike filaments that survive pureeing, so I suggest straining any mango puree before feeding it to your baby. If you can deal with the straining process, you can make a puree that your baby will love. The mango is purportedly the most widely consumed fresh fruit in the world.[2]

NUTRIENTS

Vitamin A

Vitamin B

Vitamin C

Vitamin E

Vitamin K

pure apple puree *(fall)*

This classic puree is a favorite for all ages and made even more delicious by the fact that apples are rich in vitamins A, B, and C. They also have more fiber than most cereals and breads, which is great for your baby's brand-new digestive system. A bonus: Making homemade applesauce warms your home!

NUTRIENTS

Dietary fiber

Vitamin A

Vitamin B

Vitamin C

ROOT VEGGIES

Root veggies are grown underground and as a result can be affected by impure groundwater carrying pesticides. Nonorganic root vegetables can carry high levels of nitrates, so be sure to buy organic root vegetables.

pure carrot puree *(year round)*

Carrots are a wonderful source of antioxidants and thus are super-healthy. They are fun to eat and generally available year-round. Eating carrots can help protect against heart disease and certain cancers and promote good vision. The vegetable's beta-carotene is a rich source of vitamin A.

NUTRIENTS

Antioxidants

Beta-carotene

Vitamin A

1 pound carrots

1. Wash and peel the carrots. Cut off the ends. Chop the carrots into thin rounds (½ inch thick or smaller).

2. Steam the carrot pieces for 15 to 20 minutes, or until soft (the flat side of a metal spatula will easily mash the carrots). Reserve the liquid from the steamer.

3. Transfer the steamed carrot pieces to a food processor. Add ½ cup of the reserved liquid. Puree until smooth. Continue to add the reserved liquid in scant ⅛-cup increments until the puree reaches the desired consistency and smoothness.

MAMA MANTRA

"As I make these carrots, I will put all my love into it and know that I am nuturing my baby's body, mind, and soul."

ANOTHER ROOT VEGGIES IDEA:
PREPARE THE SAME WAY AS CARROTS

pure sweet potato puree *(winter)*

Sweet potatoes are the holy grail of vegetables for babies! Sweet potato puree is a great first bite and eases the new eater into solids with delicious flavor and supernutrition. Babies really cannot get enough of this freshly steamed puree.

NOTE: Use 1 medium-size garnet yam when you make the puree. (A garnet yam will have orange flesh, not white.) I prefer garnet yams to white sweet potatoes because garnets have a higher natural water content. That said, you could use this recipe with white sweet potatoes or even regular baking potatoes.

NUTRIENTS

Antioxidants

Beta-carotene

Vitamin A

Vitamin C

LEGUMES

Legumes are essentially "pods" that open along a seam—the pod provides this superfood with a protective home while it grows. When coupled with grains, legumes form a complete protein and thus make an excellent, well-balanced meal for vegetarians.

pure green bean puree (winter)

I love green beans—and so will your baby. While quite low in calories (just 43.75 calories in a whole cup), green beans are packed with enough nutrients to power up the Jolly Green Giant and put a big smile on his face.[3]

> NUTRIENTS
> Dietary fiber
> Folate
> Vitamin A
> Vitamin C
> Vitamin K

1 pound green beans

1. Wash the green beans. Cut or snip off and discard the ends. Chop the beans into 1-inch pieces.

2. Steam the pieces for 12 to 15 minutes, or until soft (the side of a metal spatula will easily cut the beans). Reserve the liquid from the steamer.

3. Transfer the beans to a food processor. Add ¼ cup of the reserved liquid. Puree until smooth. Continue to add the reserved liquid in scant ⅛-cup increments until the puree reaches the desired consistency and smoothness.

MORE LEGUME IDEAS:
PREPARE THE SAME WAY AS GREEN BEANS

pure asparagus puree *(spring)*

Asparagus has been prized for its medicinal properties for nearly 2,000 years. Originating in the eastern Mediterranean region, this flavorful, vitamin-rich vegetable has become naturalized through- out much of the world.[4] Serving asparagus introduces your baby to an epicurean delight.

> **NUTRIENTS**
> Folate
> Vitamin A
> Vitamin C
> Vitamin K

pure pea puree *(spring)*

Peas are delicious and chock-full of nutrients. Visit your local farmers' market during the early months of spring and select from available varieties. Babies love peas, and it's always a nice feeling to see your baby gobbling up greens. Simply steam the peas for to 10 minutes, or until soft.

> **NUTRIENTS**
> Dietary fiber
> Iron
> Protein
> Vitamin C
> Vitamin K

> **MAMA MANTRA**
> *"I want my baby to grow healthly, strong, and happy!"*

SQUASHES

The colors of squash are like a brilliant fall day, ranging from rich yellows and deep oranges to many shades of green. Winter squashes are considered thick skinned and taste best when baked. Thin-skinned summer squashes can be steamed for your baby's purees.

BAKED SQUASH

pure butternut squash puree *(fall)*

Butternut squash provides 1½ times your Recommended Dietary Allowance of vitamin A and nearly half of your RDA of vitamin C.[5] It has a buttery flavor and is a wonderful first food for your baby. It also serves as a great base for more complex dishes.

> NUTRIENTS
>
> Potassium
>
> Vitamin A
>
> Vitamin C

1½ pounds butternut squash (½ medium squash)

1. Preheat the oven to 400°F.

2. Wash the butternut squash, cut off the ends, slice the squash open lengthwise, and clean out the seeds. Wrap half in plastic and store in the refrigerator.

3. Brush all sides of the remaining squash piece with olive oil. Place on a baking sheet and bake for about 1 hour, or until a sharp knife passes easily all the way through the squash.

4. Remove the squash from the oven and let cool. Peel the skin from the squash and transfer the flesh to a food processor. Add 1½ cups of purified water and puree until smooth. Continue adding water, ½ cup at a time, until the squash puree reaches the desired consistency.

ANOTHER BAKED SQUASH IDEA: PREPARE THE SAME WAY AS BUTTERNUT SQUASH

pure pumpkin puree *(fall)*

Carved pumpkins are a Halloween favorite, but the flesh of this squash can also be enjoyed in meals. Pumpkin puree is a wonderful base for baking. With its high nutritional content, pumpkin is a great, easily digestible first food for your baby.

> NUTRIENTS
> Iron
> Magnesium
> Potassium
> Vitamin A
> Vitamin C
> Vitamin K

STEAMED SQUASH

pure yellow squash puree *(summer)*

Yellow squash is easy for a new baby to digest. These bright yellow goodies are a gentle way to set your baby on his culinary path.

> NUTRIENTS
> Dietary fiber
> Protein
> Vitamin A
> Vitamin C

2 pounds yellow summer squash

1. Wash and peel the squash and cut the flesh into ½-inch-thick pieces.

2. Steam the pieces for 6 to 8 minutes, or until soft. Reserve the liquid from the steamer.

3. Transfer the squash to a food processor and puree until smooth. Add the reserved liquid (if necessary) in scant ⅛-cup increments until the puree reaches the desired consistency and smoothness.

MAMA MANTRA
"I am breathing deeply, and I am pouring good intentions into the butternut squash puree."

ANOTHER STEAMED SQUASH IDEA:
PREPARE THE SAME WAY AS YELLOW SQUASH

pure zucchini squash puree *(summer)*

Tangy zucchini has high levels of vitamin C and superantioxidants. Once your baby moves beyond purees, keep zucchini in the regular meal rotation. Zucchini is usually popular with kids, and there are infinite ways to prepare it.

NUTRIENTS

Dietary fiber

Protein

Vitamin C

SUPERGREENS

These superhealthy green purees are chock-full of the nutrition every baby needs to grow. By feeding your baby fresh green foods early and often, you'll help her develop a lifelong love of vegetables. They're great for you, too!

pure green broccoli puree *(winter)*

Even though broccoli is incredibly healthy, it is rarely a favorite with babies or older kids. It may take a few tries, but eventually, your baby will learn to love this puree. I like to call the broccoli stalks baby trees; somehow that playful name makes a difference to the toddlers I am trying to feed.

NUTRIENTS

Folate

Vitamin A

Vitamin B_1
(thiamin)

Vitamin B_2
(riboflavin)

Vitamin C

1 pound broccoli

1. Wash the broccoli and cut off the stalks. Cut the florets and stalks into 1-inch pieces.

2. Steam the pieces for 8 to 10 minutes, or until soft. Reserve the liquid from the steamer.

3. Transfer the broccoli to a food processor. Add ¼ cup of the reserved liquid. Puree until smooth. Continue to add the reserved liquid in scant ⅛-cup increments until the puree reaches the desired consistency and smoothness.

ANOTHER SUPERGREENS IDEA:
PREPARE THE SAME WAY AS BROCCOLI

pure kale puree *(winter)*

Kale is a powerhouse of nutrition! Eat it as often as you can, and encourage your kids to do the same. Kale is full of antioxidants and has cancer-fighting properties. If its flavor is too strong for your baby, mix in a little banana.

NUTRIENTS

Beta-carotene

Calcium

Vitamin C

Vitamin K

MAMA MANTRA

"When I start cooking for my baby, I will do so with care and consciousness."

PART TWO

Enlightenment

CHAPTER 6

Expanding Baby's Palate beyond Purees

Your baby is growing fast. Just as you start to get into a comfortable routine, she wants something new. This can be an exciting time! You get to be more creative with your recipes and introduce your baby to an expanding world of culinary delights.

Once your baby masters eating purees and develops the ability to chew some solid foods, it's time to infuse her diet with new textures and flavors. You will notice that your baby is starting to get curious about what you are eating. At times, you may know inherently what your baby can handle and when to introduce new foods. Trust these mothering instincts; they are unique to you and your baby! When you listen to these instincts and pay close attention to your baby's cues, the process of expanding your baby's diet will seamlessly unfold.

This is the perfect time to establish family standards and mealtime routines that include your new culinary explorer. Life can be so busy. Mealtimes are a perfect opportunity for parents and children to slow down and be together. Young babies enjoy family activities, and inviting them to participate in family meals sets up sound habits for the future. Here are a few tips to help you get started.

Establish consistent mealtimes. Babies and young toddlers crave routine. Setting consistent mealtimes helps children know what to expect. Since young children cannot tell time, their internal body clocks rely on routines for eating, playing, and sleeping. Consistent mealtimes also ensure that children will not experience abrupt changes in blood sugar levels, which can affect their behavior and cause mood swings.

Be mindful of baby's seat. Toddlers are more likely to sit and eat longer with a child-size table and chair, where their feet touch the ground, or in a high chair with a foot-rest for support. Young toddlers rarely can sit still through an hour-long meal. You can encourage your children to sit a bit longer by offering them the option to color or read at the table once they finish eating. But if they have lost interest completely, allow them to play in a nearby childproof area while you finish your meal.

Be creative. Food appearance, presentation, and packaging matter to young toddlers. If you cut sandwiches in cool shapes or serve veggies in interesting bowls, your child may be more willing to try unfamiliar foods. Take the time to add fresh flowers to the table and

let your toddlers use real cloth napkins. This will add to the aesthetic and start to teach your young children to value the natural beauty around them.

Encourage healthy snacks. Adults commonly eat three meals a day. Young children, however, should eat five small meals a day, or three meals and two snacks. Fruits and raw veggies are nutritious offerings for children in between meals.

Embrace independence. Be happy when your child shows an interest in self-feeding. Mealtimes will be a bit messier, but your child will eventually learn to feed herself neatly, and you both will have some fun along the way.

Avoid pressuring. Respect tiny tummies by letting your child eat as little or as much as he wants at each meal. Never bribe or threaten your child to "just finish the last two spoonfuls."

Avoid distraction. Allow your toddler to enjoy your full presence. Eat meals together without the distraction of newspapers, books, or television. Enjoy this time with your little one!

Focus on the flavorful. Yes, babies care about taste. But when you ask most adults what they think of baby food, you get a visceral reaction . . . *yuck!*

Many conventional baby foods sold in supermarkets do not taste good because they have been heat-treated at high temperatures. This processing allows the food to sit on a shelf without refrigeration for up to 2 years. While the heat treatment kills all potential pathogens, including bacteria that can cause spoilage, it also destroys the taste, texture, and some nutritional value of the food. If you begin to feed your baby solids at age 6 months, it is possible that the jar of conventional baby food is older than she is! Fresh seasonal foods taste great, and babies can distinguish the store-bought stuff from Mom's homemade goodness.

I have spoken with many parents who were in a panic because their children would not eat vegetables—and sometimes a child would not eat baby food at all! In every case, these parents were using commercial shelf-stable baby food. Once these parents began serving fresh foods and different flavor combinations, they saw immediate results: The babies loved their new food.

I encourage you to play with the recipes in this book to see what works and what does not work for your baby. But most of all, have fun with flavor. Don't be afraid to introduce your baby to the many spices of life!

CHAPTER 7

Special Diets
Vegetarianism, Diets for Food Allergies, and Gluten-Free Diets

VEGETARIANISM

Vegetarianism, a plant-based diet that excludes meat, is becoming increasingly popular. Vegetarian diets can reduce the risk of obesity, coronary heart disease, type 2 diabetes, hypertension, and lung cancer in children and adults. Noted pediatricians Benjamin Spock, MD,[1] and Jay Gordon, MD,[2] both advise that most children be put on vegan diets. Dr. Spock suggests vegan diets after age 2; Dr. Gordon does not advocate ever giving children dairy or meat. However, some pediatricians do not agree with these philosophies. Do the research and determine what is best for your family. Alan Greene, MD, for example, believes that "children need healthy sources of proteins, either from fish, poultry, eggs, and meat or from plant sources and that babies should not start a vegan diet until age 3–4."[3] All of the aforementioned pediatricians say babies should be breastfed for brain growth, and they also believe that extended breastfeeding past age 1 is very beneficial to the child's development.

As people become more informed about healthy ways to nourish their bodies without meat, many variations of the vegetarian diet have developed.

Vegetarians, by definition, do not eat any meat; however, many do consume eggs and dairy, a diet known as lacto-ovo vegetarianism.

Vegans do not eat any animal products, including dairy products, eggs, and honey. Many vegans are advocates for animal rights and have ethical reasons to exclude animal products from their diets.

Semivegetarianism is an increasingly popular nutrition choice. A semivegetarian diet is primarily plant based but may at times include fish, poultry, and dairy products and eggs. Pesco-vegetarianism, also called pescetarianism, is a vegetarian diet that includes fish; it's the most popular semivegetarian diet today. Noted pediatrician William Sears, MD, believes a pesco-vegetarian diet is the healthiest diet for most people.[4]

By committing to a plant-based diet for your child, you support the wise use of environmental resources. According to a study done by Andrews University, "one acre of land will support seven people if it is used to grow grains and beans for human consumption; it will support less than one person if that same acre is given over to milk and meat."[5]

Nondairy Calcium Sources for Vegetarians

Toddlers, ages 1 to 3 years, need about 500 milligrams of calcium daily. This is equivalent to two glasses of cow's milk but can also be met from nondairy calcium sources. Fortified soy milk and rice milk, calcium-fortified orange juice, black beans, vegetarian baked beans, sweet potatoes, tofu, raw broccoli, tahini, oatmeal, and almonds are all good sources of calcium.

The key to healthy vegetarian, vegan, or any diets in young children is careful planning to ensure all nutritional needs are met. All diets should give special consideration to your child's intake of calcium, iron, protein, riboflavin, vitamin A, vitamin B_2, vitamin B_{12}, vitamin D, and zinc.

FOOD ALLERGIES

Hippocrates was one of the first physicians to report an adverse reaction to milk—and that was more than 2,000 years ago. Today it is common to hear mothers comparing long lists of food allergies that they suspect plague their young children. It can be difficult to tell when children are truly allergic and when they are simply sensitive to the offending food.

A skin rash or diarrhea following the ingestion of foods such as grains or fruits is an intolerance or sensitivity. The child's digestive system may simply not be mature enough to handle the proteins, peptides, and carbohydrates in the food. This may pass as the child matures in age.

An allergic reaction is caused by the interaction between the food, the gastrointestinal tract, and the immune system in the child. Symptoms may vary. There can be an immediate reaction (within 1 hour of eating the food), or the reaction may be delayed up to 3 to 8 hours after ingestion. A reaction can be minor, such as throat or mouth irritation, or there may be stomach cramps and nausea followed by vomiting and weight loss. In more severe reactions, respiratory symptoms such as coughing or wheezing and, in some cases, more severe asthmatic symptoms may occur. The prevalence of true food allergies in the general population is only 6 to 8 percent in children less than 4 years old. This means that if you suspect your child has a food allergy, it may only be an intolerance that she will outgrow in time, usually after her third birthday. Talk to your doctor!

Adverse Food Reactions

Here are some guidelines for defining food reactions from the National Institute of Allergy and Infectious Diseases.

Food sensitivity: any abnormal response including but not limited to rashes, diarrhea, and vomiting resulting from ingesting a certain food or food additive

Food allergy: any reaction resulting from eating a food that negatively interacts with one's immune system

Food intolerance: an abnormal reaction in the digestive system response rather than an immune system response

Food Allergy Management Choices
Delay Solid Foods

Delay the introduction of solid foods until your child is at least 6 months old. Waiting lowers the incidence of serious infant illness from diarrhea. Infant digestive enzyme activity continues to mature between 4 and 6 months, which helps reduce the chance of possible food allergies. Avoid giving cow's milk and dairy products until your child is over 12 months of age.

Elimination Diet

If you suspect your child has a food sensitivity or allergy, the next step is to eliminate the food or foods from your child's diet (as well as your own, if you are still nursing). True elimination means

Many local grocery stores carry dried seaweed. You can also find it in a Japanese market or online.

Storage: Refrigerate after opening.

Wheat Germ *8+ Months*

Wheat germ is full of nutrients such as iron, vitamin B, folic acid, and vitamin E. Wheat germ helps with baby brain development and is great for adults as well! Virtually flavorless, wheat germ can be bought in granules or as a powder. A few pinches go a long way. I especially like Krestchmer brand.

Storage: Due to the natural oils found in wheat germ, it's important to store it in a glass container in the refrigerator.

Flaxseed *7+ Months*

Flaxseed contains the mighty omega-3 fatty acids. It provides extra fiber, healthy oils, and essential nutrients that enhance children's health and development. Use flaxseed that is ground to a powder for easy mix-in access.

Storage: Flaxseed should be stored in an airtight container in the refrigerator.

Açai Berries *10+ Months*

Açai, a berry native to the Amazon region of Brazil, is considered to be one of nature's most complete and healthy foods. The berry is loaded with antioxidants, amino acids, essential omegas, fiber, and protein.

Storage: Açai berries come dried. You can grind them or buy açai powder to add to your meals. Store the dried berries in your pantry. Refrigerate the powder after opening or grinding.

CHAPTER 9

Baby Blends, All-Season Cereals, and Yogurt Recipes

8 to 12 Months

baby tallulah's "spring fling" kiwifruit, pear, and raisin blend (spring)

This recipe combines the wonderful tropical flavor of kiwi with sweet pear and the slightly grainy texture of raisins. I promise that your baby will *love* this! Kiwis are packed with vitamin C and potassium.

MAKES 2 SERVINGS

2 large pears (Bartlett is best)

1 tablespoon raisins

2 kiwifruits

1. Peel and core the pears. Cut the pulp into 1-inch pieces.

2. Steam the pears and raisins together for 10 minutes, or until the pears are soft. Reserve the liquid from the steamer.

3. Peel and cut the kiwis into 1-inch pieces.

4. Combine the pears, raisins, and kiwi in a food processor. Puree until the raisins are finely chopped. Add the reserved liquid in scant ⅛-cup increments to achieve the desired consistency.

variation: pear, blueberry, and raisin blend (summer)

Blueberries are a wonderful natural antioxidant. This flavor combination is a huge hit with babies. It was my daughter's absolute favorite blend.

2 large Bartlett pears (or Anjou or other green pear)

1 tablespoon raisins

½ cup fresh blueberries

MAMA MANTRA

"My baby is growing into who she is meant to be, and I am so grateful to be her mother."

baby story's "green baby" green beans, broccoli, kale, and banana blend *(winter)*

This is a super-power-packed nutritional dynamite of a dish! Kale is full of vitamins K, A, and C. Combine this with broccoli, green beans, and the sweet taste of banana, and you have an instant winner!

MAKES 6 SERVINGS

1 cup fresh green beans

1 cup fresh broccoli florets (6 to 8 ounces)

1 cup green kale leaves (6 to 8 ounces)

3 ripe medium bananas

1. Wash the beans and cut off the ends. Cut the beans into pieces about 1 inch in length. Steam the green beans for 20 minutes, or until tender.

2. Wash and cut the broccoli in pieces 1 to 2 inches in length. Steam for 10 minutes.

3. Wash the kale, cut off the stems, and wilt the leaves in a steamer for 5 to 7 minutes. Reserve the liquid from the steamer.

4. Peel the bananas and slice into 1-inch pieces.

5. Put the beans in a food processor with ¼ cup of the reserved liquid and puree until smooth. Add more of the reserved liquid as needed to reach the desired consistency. A runny consistency is fine at this point.

6. Add the broccoli to the green bean puree. Continue to process the mixture until smooth, adding more liquid to keep the mixture from becoming too thick.

7. Add the kale leaves to the puree and continue to process, adding more liquid as needed.

8. Add the banana pieces and continue to process, adding more liquid as needed until you reach the desired consistency for your baby.

NOTE: This is a great recipe to spoon over orzo for more texture. Or serve it with any other small pasta that your baby enjoys.

MAMA MANTRA
"Preparing healthy, delicious food is my gift to my family."

baby thacher's "healthy baby" carrot, spinach, and beet blend *(summer)*

All of the ingredients in this recipe are packed with nutrients: Beets are rich in potassium, iron, and magnesium; carrots are full of beta-carotene; and spinach is loaded with fiber and iron. The more of this blend that you can encourage your baby to eat, the better!

MAKES 6 SERVINGS

3 to 4 medium carrots

1 medium beet

1 cup fresh spinach leaves (6 to 8 ounces)

1. Wash, peel, and cut the carrots into ½-inch pieces.

2. Wash, peel, and cut the beet into 1-inch pieces.

3. Steam the carrots and beet together for 20 minutes, or until soft. Reserve the liquid from the steamer.

4. Wash the spinach and remove the stems. Wilt in the steamer for about 7 minutes.

5. Add the carrots and beet and ½ cup of the reserved liquid to a food processor and puree until smooth. Add more liquid as needed to achieve the desired consistency.

6. Add the spinach to the food processor and puree until smooth, adding more reserved liquid as needed.

MAMA MANTRA

"I cook with joy."

baby remi's "tasty tart" peach and dried apricot blend

(summer)

This awesome blend is full of beta-carotene and vitamins A, B, and C. It has a pleasant, somewhat tart taste. Spoon it over alphabet pasta once your baby starts chewing. Throw in a teaspoon of wheat germ or ground flaxseed to make this dish even more nutritious.

MAKES 2 SERVINGS

1 cup dried apricots (2 or 3 apricots, depending on size)

2 large yellow peaches

1. Steam the dried apricots for 12 minutes, or until they soften and absorb some moisture.

2. Peel and pit the peaches. Cut the flesh into 1-inch pieces.

3. Steam the peaches for 8 minutes, or until they are soft. Reserve the liquid from the steamer.

4. Combine the peaches and apricots in a food processor and puree until smooth. Add the reserved liquid as needed in scant ⅛-cup increments to achieve the desired consistency.

MAMA MANTRA

"Our family meals help grow connections with each other and create lasting memories."

baby kit's "protein plus" sweet potato, spinach, and tofu blend

Little ones love this creamy, protein-packed meal. Your baby will get a healthy dose of iron, protein, vitamin A, beta-carotene, and antioxidants.

MAKES 6 SERVINGS

1 medium garnet yam (sweet potato)

1½ cups fresh spinach (about half a bunch)

¾ cup soft tofu

1. Peel and dice the yam into 1-inch pieces. Steam for 20 minutes, or until soft. Reserve the liquid from the steamer.

2. Add the yam and 1 cup of the reserved liquid to a food processor. Puree until smooth. Add more liquid as needed to achieve the desired consistency.

3. Wash the spinach and remove the stems. Wilt the leaves in the steamer for 7 minutes.

4. Add the spinach and tofu to the food processor. Puree until smooth, adding more reserved liquid as needed to reach the desired consistency.

baby happy's "harvest time" pear and pomegranate blend (fall)

The fall brings beautiful golden colors and amazing smells and flavors. Pomegranates are full of immunity-boosting antioxidants, and in the fall we all need a little help to stay healthy. This is a delicious flavor combination that babies love.

MAKES 4 SERVINGS

2 Bartlett pears

Organic pure unsweetened pomegranate juice

1. Peel, core, and cut the pears into 1-inch pieces.

2. Steam the pears for 10 minutes, or until they are soft.

3. Combine the pears and ¼ cup of the pomegranate juice in a food processor and puree until smooth. Add more juice as needed in scant ⅛-cup increments to achieve the desired consistency.

> **MAMA MANTRA**
> *"One of the greatest ways I nurture you is with a healthy variety of food."*

baby keegan's "fall warmth" apple and cranberry blend *(fall)*

The flavor of fresh cranberries makes this mixture a little tart. Cranberries are packed with vitamins A and C.

MAKES 4 TO 5 SERVINGS

½ cup fresh cranberries

4 Fuji apples

Purified water for mixing

1. Wash the cranberries and remove any stems. Steam for 3 to 5 minutes, or until the berries begin to break apart. Transfer the berries immediately to a food processor and puree, adding small amounts of liquid from the steamer to obtain a smooth, thick liquid.

2. Peel, core, and cut the apples into 1-inch pieces. Steam for 10 minutes, or until soft. Reserve the liquid from the steamer.

3. Add the apples to the cranberries with ½ cup of the reserved liquid. Puree, adding more reserved liquid as needed to obtain the desired consistency.

MAMA MANTRA

"I love you."

baby sophia's "pack 'em in" kale and sweet potato superblend *(winter)*

This is a nutritional dynamo of a dish; it couples power-packed kale with the rich, creamy taste of sweet potato. If your baby ate this dish every day, he would be in excellent nutritional shape! Add some mix-ins for a change in flavor and even more nutrition.

MAKES 5 SERVINGS

1 large garnet yam (sweet potato)

1 cup fresh kale (about 3 leaves), chopped

1. Wash, peel, and cut the yam into 1-inch pieces. Steam for 20 minutes, or until soft. Reserve the liquid from the steamer.

2. Transfer the yam to a food processor. Puree with 1½ cups of the reserved liquid, adding more liquid as needed to achieve the desired consistency.

3. Wash the kale and remove the stems. Wilt the leaves in the steamer for 7 minutes. Add the kale to the yam mixture in the food processor. Puree. Add more liquid as needed to maintain the desired consistency.

MAMA MANTRA

"We are each other's teacher. I hope you learn good eating habits from me."

"every baby's favorite" apple
and butternut squash blend *(fall)*

The creamy, buttery flavor of butternut squash combined with the fresh sweetness of apples makes this classic combination a favorite with babies. Simply combine the two purees and serve.

> 1 cup Pure Butternut Squash Puree (page 41)
>
> 1 cup Pure Apple Puree (page 36)

MAMA MANTRA

"I am so grateful to be creating the time to cook for you. It's fun and exciting."

MORE TO CHEW ON! TEXTURED MEALS

The recipes in this section are perfect for babies who are ready to move beyond smooth purees and practice chewing semisolid foods. As your baby becomes a more experienced eater, you can adjust the consistency of these meals—she will love experiencing the new textures!

baby suzie q's "orange veggie" plate with red lentils and carrots

Lentils are a legume, and like other types of beans, they contain plenty of healthy nutrients, including dietary fiber, iron, and protein. Babies are intrigued by the bright orange color of this dish.

MAKES 6 SERVINGS

1 cup red lentils

3½ cups purified water

2 cups Pure Carrot Puree (page 37)

1. Wash the lentils and remove any debris and discolored or deformed beans.

2. Combine the lentils and purified water in a medium saucepan. Bring to a boil. Reduce the heat and simmer for 10 minutes, or until the lentils are tender. The lentils will turn a lighter orange color, the beans will split open, and the mixture will thicken to the consistency of runny oatmeal. Do not strain.

3. Combine 2 cups of the cooked lentils with the carrot puree. Whisk the mixture until uniformly combined.

MAMA MANTRA

"I am learning and growing with my baby, and every day I see the world with new eyes."

baby rio's "enlightenment" eggplant and red bell pepper puree with red lentils *(summer)*

Eggplant is a meaty vegetable that can be cooked in many ways. This tasty recipe is full of protein, fiber, vitamins A and C, and folic acid, making it a powerhouse of nutrition.

MAKES 4 SERVINGS

1 medium eggplant, peeled and cut into pieces

1 red bell pepper, seeded and diced

1 cup red lentils

1 garlic clove, minced

3½ cups purified water

1 teaspoon flaxseed

1. Preheat the oven to 350°F.

2. Drizzle olive oil on a baking sheet. Place the eggplant and pepper on the sheet and mix together. Bake for 12 minutes, or until soft.

3. Place the eggplant and pepper in a food processor. Puree. Set aside.

4. Wash the lentils and remove any debris and discolored or deformed beans. Combine the lentils, garlic, and purified water in a medium saucepan. Bring to a boil. Reduce the heat and simmer for 10 minutes, or until the lentils are tender. The lentils will turn a lighter orange color, the beans will split open, and the mixture will thicken to the consistency of runny oatmeal. Do not strain.

5. Combine 2 cups of the lentil mix with 2 cups of the eggplant/bell pepper puree. Add the flaxseed. Mix well.

6. If your baby still needs completely pureed food, put the entire mixture back in the food processor to blend to a pureed consistency. If your baby is eating textured foods, leave it as is.

baby maya's "tropical dream" papaya, mango, banana, and cottage cheese blend

Papaya is high in good fats needed for baby brain development, and it's gentle on the tummy. You can puree this blend to a smooth consistency or keep it a little textured so your baby can practice chewing.

MAKES 6 SERVINGS

1 large ripe papaya

1 large ripe mango

1 large ripe banana, peeled

1 cup cottage cheese

1. Wash the papaya, cut it in half lengthwise, and scoop out the seeds. Peel the skin and cut the flesh into 1-inch pieces.

2. Wash, peel, and core the mango. Cut the flesh into 1-inch pieces.

3. If the papaya and mango are very ripe and soft, then you can use them raw; otherwise, steam them for 7 minutes, or until soft (cooking time will depend on ripeness).

4. Transfer the papaya, mango, and banana to a food processor. Puree, adding water as needed to obtain the desired consistency.

5. Fold the cottage cheese into the fruit mixture and serve.

MAMA MANTRA

"I love this culinary adventure we are on together."

baby grant's "conscious surprise" fuji apple, butternut squash, dried cranberries, and couscous blend *(fall)*

Couscous is quick, light, and fluffy. Most babies like its texture. This recipe offers a little sweet and a little savory to your baby's palate and helps her practice eating textured food.

MAKES 5 SERVINGS

1 tablespoon sweetened dried cranberries

1 cup Pure Apple Puree (page 36)

1 cup Pure Butternut Squash Puree (page 41)

1 cup plain couscous

1. Steam the cranberries for about 10 minutes.

2. Combine the apple and butternut squash purees and cranberries in a food processor. Chop until the purees are fully mixed and the cranberries are finely chopped.

3. Prepare the couscous according to package directions and fold into the apple/butternut squash mixture.

MAMA MANTRA

"I am so glad we were led to each other. You are the most amazing baby, and I am in awe of what you teach me every day."

baby daniel's "pumpkin and root veggies" combo of roasted pumpkin, carrots, and yellow potatoes *(fall)*

Nothing says "home" like the delicious fragrance of roasting root vegetables in autumn. You will love the simplicity of this recipe; your baby will love the taste. Feel free to substitute some of your favorite veggies for those I have chosen.

MAKES 5 SERVINGS

1 pie pumpkin

2 jumbo carrots

3 small Yukon Gold potatoes

2 shallots

1 garlic clove

4 tablespoons olive oil

Sea salt and pepper to taste

1. Preheat the oven to 400°F. Grease the bottom of a 9 × 11-inch glass baking dish with olive oil.

2. Wash the pie pumpkin, cut it in half, and scoop out the seeds. Cut the flesh into 1-inch cubes, leaving the skin on. Transfer the flesh to a large mixing bowl.

3. Wash and peel the carrots. Slice into 1-inch pieces and add to the pumpkin.

4. Wash the potatoes. Cut into 1-inch pieces, leaving the skin on. Add to the pumpkin mixture.

5. Cut the shallots in half, remove the skin, and add to the pumpkin mixture.

6. Peel the garlic clove. Quarter it and add to the pumpkin mixture.

7. Sprinkle the vegetable mixture with the oil and toss to coat the vegetables completely. Add a few pinches of salt and pepper to taste.

8. Place the vegetables in a single layer in the baking dish. Bake on the center rack of the oven for 10 minutes. Stir the vegetables, redistribute them in a single layer, and roast for an additional 10 minutes, or until all of the vegetables are soft.

9. The cooked vegetables can be either mashed or pureed to suit your baby. Serve warm.

baby eliza's "tart compote" of apples, soft chunky carrots, and butternut squash *(fall)*

Apples give this compote its sweet flavor, which most babies appreciate. Coupled with carrot and butternut squash, this apple dish makes a warming, nourishing meal. When your baby gets a little older, try serving this compote with brown rice mixed in.

MAKES 4 SERVINGS

1 jumbo carrot

1 cup Pure Apple Puree, made with Granny Smith apples (page 36)

1 cup Pure Butternut Squash Puree (page 37)

1. Wash and peel the carrot and remove the ends. Cut the carrot lengthwise into quarters and slice into ⅛-inch pieces. Steam the carrot pieces for 15 minutes, or until soft.

2. Combine the apple and butternut squash purees and whisk until fully mixed.

3. Fold in the carrot pieces.

baby tara's "winter goodness" yellow squash, carrot, apple, and broccoli blend *(winter)*

This combination joins healthy veggies with a hint of apple sweetness. Your baby will not only enjoy the flavors but have a healthy meal that you can feel good about feeding her.

MAKES 4 SERVINGS

2 medium yellow squash

1 apple

2 large carrots

2 stalks broccoli (or 4 broccoli florets)

1. Wash the squash and remove the ends. Cut the flesh into ¼-inch-thick slices. Peel and chop the apple and add to the squash. Steam together for 7 minutes, or until soft. Reserve the liquid from the steamer.

2. Wash and peel the carrots. Slice into ¼-inch-thick slices. Steam for 20 minutes, or until soft. Reserve the liquid.

3. Wash the broccoli and cut into 1- to 2-inch pieces. Steam for 10 minutes. Reserve the liquid.

4. Combine the squash/apple mixture, carrots, and broccoli in a food processor. Puree, adding some of the reserved liquid to obtain the desired consistency.

MAMA MANTRA

"Sharing life with you is pure happiness."

baby eva's "sweet and savory" green lentil, sweet potato, and broccoli blend

You can add a shot of wheat germ for an extra nutritional burst to this tasty recipe.

MAKES 6 SERVINGS

1 cup green lentils

1 large garnet yam (sweet potato)

2 stalks broccoli (or 4 broccoli florets)

1. Wash the lentils and remove any debris or deformed beans. Bring 1½ cups of water to a boil in a medium saucepan. Add the lentils, boil for 3 minutes, then reduce the heat and simmer for 45 minutes, or until the lentils are soft. Remove from the heat.

2. Wash, peel, and cut the yam into 1-inch pieces. Steam for 20 minutes, or until soft. Reserve the liquid from the steamer.

3. Transfer the yam to a food processor. Puree with 1½ cups of the reserved liquid, adding more liquid as needed to achieve the desired consistency.

4. Wash the broccoli and cut into 1- to 2-inch pieces. Steam for 10 minutes. Add to the yam in the food processor. Continue to puree, adding more reserved liquid as needed to reach the desired consistency. Add the lentils to the food processor. Puree until the blend is well mixed and an appropriate consistency for your baby.

PAPA MANTRA

"Being your daddy has changed my life and the way I see the world. I am grateful for that."

ORGANIC BREAKFAST CEREALS AND GRAINS

These breakfast cereals are the perfect way to introduce your baby to whole grains. Plain whole grains can be a bit bland, so I like to combine them with the purees from Chapter 5 for extra flavor and nutrients. Your baby will love these yummy, gentle cereals so much that you won't ever have to buy the boxed stuff!

baby megan's "awaken" pear, raisins, and millet cereal

Millet is an easy-to-digest supergrain—a wonderful first grain for babies. It has a mild flavor, and babies enjoy the texture. The taste of the raisins in this meal is the ticket. You can also add a shot of a healthy mix-in to change it up. Your baby will inhale this classic breakfast meal!

MAKES 8 SERVINGS

½ cup millet

2 tablespoons raisins

2 cups Pure Pear Puree (page 34)

1. Grind the millet to a fine powder in a small coffee grinder.
2. Bring 2 cups of water to a boil in a medium saucepan. Add the millet powder and whisk constantly, cooking for 7 to 10 minutes, or until thickened. Set aside.
3. Steam the raisins for 10 minutes, or until soft.
4. Combine the raisins and millet with the pear puree in a food processor. Process until the raisins are finely chopped and the mixture is uniform.

variation: millet cereal with banana and wheat germ

½ cup millet

3 large ripe bananas (about 1 pound)

2 teaspoons wheat germ

baby willow's "good morning, baby" classic apple and oats cereal

Oats are a classic breakfast treat for everyone. When you buy fresh whole grain oats and prepare them in this recipe, you maximize all of the oats' potential nutritional value for your baby. Whole grains provide carbohydrates, which are the body's main source of energy. Your baby will love this warm, sweet breakfast.

MAKES 6 SERVINGS

½ cup rolled oats

2 cups Pure Apple Puree (page 36)

1. Grind the oats to a fine powder in a small coffee grinder.

2. Bring 2 cups of water to a boil in a medium saucepan. Add the oat powder and whisk constantly, cooking for 7 to 10 minutes, or until thickened.

3. Combine the oats with the apple puree in a mixing bowl. Whisk until the mixture is uniform.

MAMA MANTRA

"Every day is filled with new opportunities to show you my love."

baby calina's "simply delicious" apple, blueberry, granola, and oats cereal

This warming cereal is so good that it will quickly become a favorite of mamas and daddies as well as baby. The flavor combination is sweet and scrumptious. This dish delivers the proteins and vitamins that your baby needs to have a productive day.

MAKES 5 SERVINGS

½ **cup fresh blueberries**

⅔ **cup nut-free granola (or include nuts if you are sure your baby has no nut allergies)**

2 **cups Classic Apple and Oats Cereal (page 85)**

1. Wash the blueberries. Steam for 3 to 5 minutes, or until the berries begin to break apart. Transfer immediately to a mixing bowl.

2. Combine the granola, cereal, and blueberries in a food processor. Puree until the granola is finely chopped and incorporated into the mixture.

MAMA MANTRA

"There is nothing that brings me more happiness than seeing you smile."

PART THREE

New Horizons

CHAPTER **10**

The Adventurous Eater

Toddlers are at an exciting and adventurous age. Now you can offer them more complex flavors and variety! Toddlers' tastebuds change just as quickly as their moods, and they may like something one day and not like it the next. This is a natural part of the experimentation typical at this stage. Always reintroduce old favorites and offer new foods several times before drawing conclusions about what your child does and does not like.

FEEDING TODDLERS AND PRESCHOOLERS

Between the ages of 1 and 5, your child's growth slows. His need for calories subsequently decreases, which in turn leads to a smaller quantity of food ingested each day. Rest assured that toddlers do not need as much food as you might expect. Three small meals and two snacks a day (and sometimes a good bit less) will be enough to fuel even the most active toddler.

Some toddlers eat very few solids, or even no solids, at 12 months. This is not unusual—toddler appetites can vary dramatically. Some children have food sensitivities, which may be the body's way of protecting the digestive system until it can handle more complex foods. Other toddlers are late teethers or have a lot of difficulty with teething pain. For many nursing toddlers, breast milk still makes up the majority (around 75 percent) of their diet at 12 months.[1] It is normal for nursing toddlers to keep breast milk as the primary component of their diet until 18 months. My friend Betsy worried because her 18-month-old daughter Josie was mostly refusing textured foods, but Josie was still happily eating purees. Many babies struggle with the various textures of solid food, and it is fine if they continue eating softer foods as they grow into being a toddler. Start very small and eventually, they will get it!

Your breast milk contains everything that your child needs, with the possible exception of iron and vitamin D. As long as your toddler's iron levels are within a healthy range and you are offering him foods naturally rich in iron, then you don't need to worry about the amount of solids he's getting. To provide vitamin D, simply make sure your toddler plays a

lot in the sunshine! If you are not nursing, it is wise to consult your child's pediatrician to ensure that adequate formula, milk, or vitamins are provided to fill any gaps. Your true responsibility lies in what you offer your child, when you offer it, and how you offer it—not whether or not he eats it. That is up to him. Trying to force, coax, or persuade your toddler to eat is never recommended.

SAMPLING THE CULTURAL CAFÉ

In my experience, feeding toddlers and preschoolers is exhilarating. They have no preconceived ideas about what they like and don't like, so they are willing participants in new culinary experiences. Every toddler should have the opportunity to try diverse spices, herbs, rich flavors, and exciting combinations of textures and colors. Offering international cuisine to babies and young children will help them develop a more mature palate, leading to a healthier relationship with food as they grow. I created the Cultural Café menu using recipes inspired by different world regions and cultures to introduce babies and toddlers to international flavors. I encourage parents to be adventurous eaters, too, as it will likely lead to their children exploring a wider range of foods.

It is okay to introduce young children to spices that have a little kick. When I make Indian food for toddlers, I am often asked whether toddlers can really handle all of those spices. I answer with a simple yes and then follow up with a discussion about what toddlers in India eat daily. I believe that we are far more conservative in America when it comes to introducing foods from other cultures to babies and toddlers. You will be surprised by how many flavors your young children will love when given the opportunity. Not only will they

6. Combine the dry and wet ingredients with a whisk, leaving the batter a little lumpy.

7. Melt the butter in a heated skillet. Pour the batter in the skillet to make 4-inch pancakes.

8. When the pancakes start to bubble a bit, flip them. Be careful not to flip too soon or you will create a big batter mess.

9. Serve warm with the blueberry syrup.

Note: You can prepare this syrup recipe with your other favorite fruits; it is especially tasty made with fresh berries.

MAMA MANTRA

"I can start my daughter's day on a positive note by making a breakfast full of good intentions and positive energy."

anni marie's famous italian tomato-basil feta scramble

This gourmet version of traditional scrambled eggs is easy, quick, and delicious. It's a protein-rich breakfast that everyone can enjoy.

MAKES 2 TO 3 SERVINGS

3 eggs

¼ cup milk

¼ cup feta cheese

4 fresh basil leaves

12 baby grape tomatoes, cut in half

½ tablespoon butter

Pinch of salt

2 pinches of black pepper

Dash of garlic salt

1. Crack the eggs in a bowl and whisk together. Whisk in the milk. Add the feta cheese; set the mixture aside.

2. Chop the basil finely. Dice the tomatoes halves. Add the basil and tomatoes to the egg mixture.

3. Melt the butter in a heated skillet. Pour in the egg mixture and start stirring to scramble the eggs. Add the salt, pepper, and garlic salt to taste.

4. When the eggs are fully cooked, remove them from the skillet. Serve warm with your choice of toast or a bagel and chopped fruit.

Mama Tip: I like to serve this with almond or plain buttered wheat toast or a cream cheese bagel.

MAMA MANTRA

"I am honored to be your mother."

jenny's easy cheesy egg soufflés

This simple, savory recipe is my mom's favorite. Make the stuffing from scratch or use a boxed mix. Kids love this bubbly, cheesy dish because they get their own individual serving portion, so it feels very fancy. Watch your toddlers dig in—you'll quickly follow suit!

MAKES 6 SERVINGS

Stuffing

¼ cup butter

½ cup onion, chopped

½ cup celery, chopped

1 garlic clove, minced

1 teaspoon ground flaxseed

½ teaspoon fresh sage, chopped

3 cups dry sourdough bread cubes

¼ cup vegetable broth

½ teaspoon fine-grain sea salt

½ teaspoon freshly ground black pepper

Soufflés

6 eggs

½ cup shredded Monterey Jack cheese

½ cup mild Cheddar cheese

½ cup sour cream

1. Preheat the oven to 400°F. Coat a large muffin pan with organic canola oil.

2. To make the stuffing: Melt the butter in a skillet. Add the onion, celery, garlic, flaxseed, and sage. Cook until the onion is soft and caramelized. Add the bread cubes, broth, salt, and pepper. Stir until combined. Remove from the heat and set aside.

3. To make the soufflés: Press the stuffing mixture in the bottom and along the side of each prepared muffin cup. Crack an egg in the bottom of each stuffing-lined muffin cup. Sprinkle each with a generous portion of the Monterey Jack and Cheddar.

4. Bake for 20 minutes, or until the middle has set. Let the soufflés stand for 5 minutes before serving. Serve each with a dollop of the sour cream as a dipping sauce.

> **MAMA MANTRA**
> *"I want my child to grow healthy, strong, and happy!"*

zoë's sweet potato fries with ponzu dipping sauce

Sweet potatoes are a superfood. A wonderful step beyond sweet potato puree, these fries are still soft and easy to chew. Toddlers feel grown up because they are now eating fries! Even older kids will gobble these up: My 12-year-old Zoë loves this snack. He says it's all about the dipping sauce!

MAKES 3 SERVINGS

Ponzu Dipping Sauce

¼ cup low-sodium soy sauce

2 garlic cloves

Splash of white distilled vinegar

Freshly ground black pepper

Fries

1 fresh garnet yam (sweet potato)

Splash of olive oil

Pinch of fine-grain sea salt

Freshly ground black pepper

2 pinches of wheat germ (optional)

1. To make the dipping sauce: Pour the soy sauce in a small glass bowl. Peel and cut open the garlic cloves. Put the cloves in the soy sauce. Add the vinegar and mix. Add pepper to taste. Set aside to give the flavors time to blend before serving.

2. To make the fries: Preheat the oven to 400°F. Peel the sweet potato and cut into fries.

3. Pour enough oil in a plastic bag to coat the fries evenly. Add the salt, pepper, and wheat germ, if using. Place the sweet potato pieces in the bag. Shake until the fries are evenly coated.

4. Spread the coated fries in a glass baking dish. Bake on one side for 10 minutes, then turn the fries and bake for another 8 minutes.

5. Serve warm with the dipping sauce.

> **MAMA MANTRA**
> *"Creativity is my secret weapon in offering healthy foods that taste delicious!"*

ocean's japanese miso soup with scallions, mushrooms, and tofu

Miso soup is a favorite in my home; my kids love it as a snack. You can change this recipe by adding different vegetables or keep it simple and traditional. Served with a little brown rice as a side dish, miso soup is the perfect quick lunch or dinner on a cold night. The ingredients may be available at your local health food store, but it's more fun to shop for them at a Japanese grocer or specialty store.

MAKES 4 SERVINGS

3 cups dashi soup stock

¾ cup firm tofu, drained and cubed into small bites

¼ cup scallions, chopped

¼ cup shiitake mushrooms, chopped

1 teaspoon dried seaweed, minced (optional)

3 tablespoons miso paste

Splash of low-sodium soy sauce or liquid amino acids (such as Bragg Liquid Aminos)

1. Pour the stock into a medium saucepan. Heat over medium heat. Add the tofu, scallions, mushrooms, and seaweed, if using. Simmer for 5 minutes.

2. Place 1 cup of the warm soup stock in a bowl. Add the miso paste and let it dissolve. Return the mixture to the saucepan.

3. Add soy sauce or Bragg's to taste. Serve warm.

MAMA MANTRA

"I can positively affect my toddler's mood by preparing this soup with a peaceful frame of mind."

duke's delicious mozzarella bruschetta

This classic dish is easy to prepare. You can make a little extra topping and save it to use over pasta or even as a dip. The key to this recipe is using fresh ingredients. Take a trip to your local farmers' market for some big bunches of organic basil and sweet grape tomatoes. Better yet, grow your own!

MAKES 10 SERVINGS

¼ cup olive oil

1 basket (6 ounces) sweet grape tomatoes, cut into quarters

Handful of fresh basil leaves, chopped

2 garlic cloves, minced

¼ cup balsamic vinegar

Pinch of fine-grain sea salt

2 pinches of freshly ground black pepper

1 ball fresh mozzarella

1 loaf fresh ciabatta bread

1. Preheat the oven to 350°F.

2. Mix the oil, tomatoes, basil, garlic, vinegar, salt, and pepper in a shallow glass baking dish. Set aside.

3. Pull off pieces of the mozzarella ball and set aside.

4. Slice the bread and lay the slices on a baking sheet. Place a piece of cheese on top of each bread slice. Top with the tomato mixture. Bake for 8 minutes, or until the cheese has melted nicely.

5. When serving a toddler, you may want to cut the bruschetta into strips. Preschoolers can handle a whole slice. (These strips also make a great appetizer for a dinner party.)

MAMA MANTRA

"Preparing fresh, organic foods from scratch helps my son grow to his full potential."

6. Spread the pieces on a baking sheet; do not overlap. (This recipe will make about 3 batches, depending on the size of your baking sheets.) Bake for 7 to 8 minutes, or until the chips are lightly golden. They will harden up a bit once they hit the air, but they should still be relatively soft when you eat them. Serve warm with the fresh guacamole.

lotus's fig spread on toasted bread with warm honey drizzle

This recipe, a variation of Parmesan garlic bread, uses sweet figs. My children love, love, love this! This snack was inspired by my daughter, who enjoys picking figs off the tree and helping me devise recipes for them. Figs are rich in potassium and dietary fiber. They are naturally sweet and, when bought in season, taste spectacular.

MAKES 8 SERVINGS

1 package dried figs or 6 fresh figs (if in season), stems removed, flesh cut and quartered

2 tablespoons lemon juice

1½ cups water

2 tablespoons agave nectar

Sourdough bread, sliced

¼ cup organic honey

1. Place the figs, lemon juice, water, and agave in a medium saucepan. Bring to a boil. Reduce the heat and simmer uncovered until the mixture thickens.

2. Remove the pan from the heat. Let the spread cool. Store it in a glass jar in the fridge for up to 4 weeks.

3. Spread the fig mixture on top of the bread slices. Bake in a toaster oven for approximately 3 minutes.

4. Heat the honey in a small saucepan. Drizzle the warm honey over the toasted bread. Let the bread cool and cut into strips for your little ones.

Mama Wisdom: "I have noticed that my daughter is more likely to eat something if she shares it with a playmate. Sharing healthy meals is a great idea."

mackenzie's superstar sweet potato cakes with sour cream

Every toddler and grown-up who has ever tasted these cakes absolutely loves them. Made from the delicious sweet potato, the cakes melt in the mouth. These are even great cold the next day or as a midnight snack for a breastfeeding mama!

MAKES 8 SERVINGS

1 medium garnet yam (sweet potato)

4 Yukon Gold potatoes or 2 large russet potatoes

1 tablespoon olive oil

1 large yellow onion, diced

¼ teaspoon salt

⅛ teaspoon freshly ground black pepper

1 teaspoon wheat germ

2 garlic cloves, minced

2 eggs

2 tablespoons heavy whipping cream

¼ cup grated Parmesan cheese

¼ cup grated Romano cheese

3 tablespoons unbleached or all-purpose flour

1. Peel and dice the potatoes and place them in a pot of cold water. Bring to a boil. Reduce the heat and simmer for 30 minutes, or until thoroughly cooked. Drain the potatoes and let them cool.

2. Peel and dice the yam into 1-inch pieces. Steam the yams for 20 minutes, or until soft.

3. Place the yams and potatoes in a large bowl. Mash until well mixed and only a little lumpiness remains. Set aside.

4. Heat the oil in a medium skillet over low heat. Add the onion, salt, pepper, and wheat germ. Cook until the onion is soft and begins to brown. Add the garlic and cook 1 minute more. Remove from the heat. Add to the potato mixture.

5. Beat the eggs and cream together in a mixing bowl. Stir them into the potato mixture along with the cheeses and flour.

6. Heat a nonstick skillet over medium-high heat or set a nonstick electric skillet to 375°F. Flatten 1 heaping tablespoon of batter into a round cake and place in the skillet. Repeat with the remaining batter. Cook the cakes for 5 minutes per side, or until a brown crust forms on each side.

7. Serve warm with a dollop of sour cream as a dipping sauce.

fiona's butternut squash with orzo

This savory dish is loaded with vitamins A and C and potassium. Even a baby just starting to chew can enjoy it. The beautiful yellow color is stimulating for little ones. It reminds me of the coziness of fall.

MAKES 3 SERVINGS

4 cups vegetable broth

½ cup orzo

1 cup Pure Butternut Squash Puree (page 41)

1. Pour the broth into a medium saucepan and heat to a rolling boil. Add the orzo and reduce the heat. Simmer for 8 to 10 minutes, or until tender.

2. Strain the orzo through a colander, but do not rinse it with water.

3. Fold ½ cup of the cooked orzo into the butternut squash puree. Serve warm. Save leftover orzo for a butter and Parmesan pasta lunch the next day

MAMA MANTRA

"In the fall, we celebrate the harvests of the year. This food is bountiful and delicious."

Mama Tip: You can vary the ratio of pasta to puree depending on how adept your baby is at chewing solid foods. The vegetable broth adds a lot of flavor to the pasta, so feel free to pour a bit more broth into the final mixture. One butternut squash makes a lot of puree, so make some extra to serve as a side dish for adults—they love it, too!

eva's spicy tomato-basil sauce with chicken and penne

This classic Italian dish is so easy to make, and everyone loves the fresh flavors. You can easily adjust the spice level of this dish depending on who will eat it.

MAKES 4 SERVINGS

3 cups penne pasta

¼ cup olive oil

4 garlic cloves, chopped fine

2 large whole tomatoes, cut in half

1 cup fresh basil leaves, roughly chopped

½ teaspoon salt

Freshly ground black pepper

½ teaspoon red pepper flakes

Juice of ½ lime

1 organic, hormone-free chicken breast, cut into bite-size pieces

¼ cup freshly grated Parmigiano-Reggiano cheese

1. Prepare the pasta according to package directions. Drain and set aside.

2. Pour the oil in a hot skillet. Reduce the heat to medium high. Add the garlic and cook for about 1 minute. Add the tomatoes, basil, salt, black and red pepper to taste, lime juice, and chicken. Stir. Cook for 7 minutes, turning each piece of chicken a few times.

3. Reduce the heat to low and simmer the chicken and sauce for 7 more minutes, stirring periodically, until the tomatoes are soft.

4. Mash the tomatoes into the sauce. Add the pasta and mix well.

5. Garnish with the cheese and serve immediately.

Mama Tip: The key to this dish is the fresh basil leaves! Either pick basil straight from your garden or buy it fresh from your local farmers' market or grocer. Remember to prepare your pasta first and set it aside while you are making the sauce and chicken.

MAMA MANTRA

"Someday I will take you to Italy to taste the true flavors of such a rich and flavorful country."

ginger's asian stir-fry

This healthy, easy dish explodes with yummy veggies and superfoods like kale and broccoli. I make this recipe at least once a week. My son Zoë always shouts "Yes!" as soon as I tell him I am cooking stir-fry for dinner. Serve this dish with Simple Brown Rice (opposite) and it will quickly become one of your family favorites, too.

MAKES 5 SERVINGS

1 tablespoon butter

2 cups chopped broccoli

1 cup chopped fresh tomatoes

2 green zucchini, chopped

Handful of snap peas

1 can (15 ounces) baby corn, chopped

½ cup chopped kale

½ cup chopped carrots

¾ cup chopped mushrooms (any variety)

3 tablespoons toasted sesame oil

3 tablespoons low-sodium soy sauce

2 pinches of ground red pepper

Garlic salt (about 2 shakes)

Freshly ground black pepper

1 tablespoon sesame seeds

1. Melt the butter in a wok or large skillet over medium heat. Add the broccoli, tomatoes, zucchini, snap peas, corn, kale, carrots, and mushrooms. Stir for a minute or two, then add the oil, soy sauce, red pepper, and garlic salt and black pepper to taste. Continue to cook over medium heat for 5 minutes, stirring constantly.

2. Reduce the heat to low and cook for another 5 minutes or so.

3. Garnish with sesame seeds. Serve immediately with Simple Brown Rice.

simple brown rice

Brown rice makes the perfect complement to Ginger's Asian Stir-Fry (opposite) and Maya-sita's Cuban Black Beans (page 157). Brown rice can be temperamental, however, so time it carefully. Start cooking the rice before you prepare the companion dish so that the two are ready at the same time.

MAKES 4 SERVINGS

3 cups brown rice

2 eggs

6 cups water

1 tablespoon olive oil, plus more as needed

3 garlic cloves, cut open and left large

1. Preheat the oven to 350°F.

2. Heat some oil in a skillet. Once the oil is hot, pour in the rice and crack the eggs right into the pan. Stir until the eggs are scrambled with the rice and the mixture appears dry.

3. Transfer the rice mixture to a glass baking dish. Cover with the water and 1 tablespoon oil. Stir in the garlic.

4. Place the baking dish in the oven and bake uncovered for 30 minutes. Open the oven, cover the rice with foil, and bake for another 30 minutes. Do not stir.

5. Check the rice after it has cooked for 1 hour. If all the water is absorbed, the rice is done. If not, return the dish to the oven until cooking is complete.

6. Transfer the rice to a bowl and remove the garlic cloves, if you wish. Serve immediately with the main course.

MAMA MANTRA

"By incorporating foods from around the world, I can expand my child's horizons and open a window for learning opportunities."

piper's teriyaki chicken sushi rolls

Japanese-style cooking is elegant and sleek. Making sushi rolls introduces your toddler not only to new flavors but to Japanese culture as well. I love it when I can teach my children something without really trying! Once you master the art of making Japanese sushi rice, which is not too tough, the whole family can have fun coming up with different sushi recipe combinations.

MAKES 4 SERVINGS

Rice with Tezu

4 cups water

4 tablespoons rice vinegar

3 tablespoons raw sugar

1 teaspoon sea salt, plus a dash

2 cups Japanese short-grain white rice

Chicken

Dash of salt

Dash of freshly ground black pepper

2 organic, hormone-free chicken breasts

4 tablespoons olive oil

2 cups teriyaki sauce (use your favorite brand), heated

5 lemon slices

Roll

Seaweed sheets

1 tablespoon sesame seeds

1 avocado, thinly sliced

1 cucumber, peeled and sliced into strips

1. To make the tezu sauce: Bring 2 cups of water and the rice vinegar to a boil in a saucepan. Add the sugar and 1 teaspoon salt. Mix until the sugar dissolves. Remove the pan from the heat and set aside.

2. Clean the rice by putting it in water and draining. Repeat several times, until the water is close to clear. Pour the cleaned rice in a saucepan. Add the remaining 2 cups of water and a dash of salt and bring to a boil. Immediately reduce the heat to low. Cover the pan and cook for 10 minutes, or until the water evaporates and the rice is sticky.

3. Spread the rice on a flat surface. Drizzle the tezu sauce over the rice. Gently mix in the tezu by folding the rice with a wooden spoon or by lightly patting the rice with your hands.

Mama Tip: To make sushi, you will need plastic wrap and a bamboo place mat that you can roll. Most of the recipe ingredients are probably available at your local supermarket, but if you have a Japanese grocer nearby, shop there! It's exciting to buy cultural foods from the source.

vaughn's grilled shrimp and veggies

Serve this simple dish on a summer's night, along with wild rice and corn on the cob. Toddlers like food that looks fun to eat, and food on a stick is not only fascinating, it's new to them.

MAKES 4 SERVINGS

1½ cups olive oil

1 cup cilantro, chopped

½ teaspoon freshly ground black pepper

2 dashes of salt

2 garlic cloves, minced

2 dashes of ground red pepper

3 lemons (1 cut in half for the juice and peel)

2 pounds fresh, deveined, uncooked shrimp

1 whole yellow onion

2 whole tomatoes

1 whole red pepper

1. To prepare the marinade: Pour the oil into a glass baking dish. Add the cilantro, black pepper, salt, garlic, red pepper, and the juice and peel of 1 lemon. Stir the mixture together. Refrigerate.

2. Put the shrimp in a colander and rinse with cold running water. Toss the shrimp in the marinade and refrigerate.

3. To prepare the skewers: Preheat the grill to medium. Cut the onion, tomatoes, bell pepper, and remaining lemons into chunks large enough for skewering. Remove the marinating shrimp from the refrigerator and start to assemble the skewers. The order can be whatever you like, but I like to do a shrimp, then a few chunks of onion, tomato, lemon, and finally the bell pepper. Reserve the marinade.

4. Place your assembled skewers on the grill. Cook for 4 or 5 minutes per side, basting the shrimp with the reserved marinade.

Note: You will need wooden skewers for this dish.

MAMA MANTRA

"Delicious food is my gift to you."

asher loves italian pasta marinara

This recipe is convenient to have on hand. You can make this dish a little spicy, depending on tolerance levels of your family members. But even when mild, this pasta has great flavor and makes a hearty meal for everyone.

MAKES 4 SERVINGS

1 can (32 ounces) stewed tomatoes

2 Roma tomatoes, chopped

1 tablespoon fresh oregano, chopped

2 tablespoon fresh basil, chopped

2 pinches of ground red pepper

Salt

Freshly ground black pepper

3 pinches of any other Italian spices you like

Splash of olive oil

1 medium onion, chopped

1 tablespoon capers

2 garlic cloves, minced

2 cups whole wheat alphabet pasta

½ cup grated Parmesan cheese

1. Combine the stewed and Roma tomatoes, oregano, basil, red pepper, salt and black pepper to taste, and any other spices in a large saucepan. Stir and cook over medium heat for 3 minutes, then reduce the heat to low.

2. Pour a little olive oil in a skillet. Add the onion, capers, and garlic. Cook until the onion is caramelized. Add to the tomato sauce. Continue to simmer the sauce on low.

3. Prepare the pasta according to the package directions. Drain and place the pasta in a serving dish. Pour the sauce over the pasta, mix, and top with the cheese. Serve immediately.

Mama Tip: This recipe suggests using wheat alphabet pasta so that even chewing babies of 8+ months can enjoy this dish. If your toddler has outgrown alphabet pasta, try this recipe with spaghetti—or make both types of pasta for all to enjoy.

MAMA MANTRA

"Encouraging my preschooler to include herbs from her herb garden in our everyday meals allows us to connect and me to nourish her inner foodie."

PART FOUR

·•·

Nirvana

CHAPTER 12

Sweets and Snacks

Everybody likes a sweet treat now and then, and your children will be no exception. As your baby grows into a toddler and preschooler and starts spending more time in the world outside your home, he will come across sugar and sweets everywhere! It's hard to manage your child's consumption of sugar when he starts going to play dates and birthday parties. He will notice the cake and other sweets available, and—plain and simple—he will want some. So what should you do? My honest advice is to let your children participate in the celebratory event. If that means allowing them to have some sugary cake, so be it. I think moderation is the key.

If you want to limit sugar intake at home, you can prepare plenty of sweet treat alternatives. The dishes in this section are nice to enjoy at home, take with you on the go, or even bring along to a party. Healthy treats still taste scrumptious. Your child will love them, and you won't have to worry about the effects of a sugar overload on his moods, diet, energy level, and overall health.

OVERCOMING THE JUNK-FOOD NATION

Today, many of our long-standing food traditions have been lost, giving way to a fast-food culture that values only speed and ease of preparation. The result in the United States has been a diet of high-fat, high-sugar food. Eating commercial fast food can

become addictive. Ultimately, consuming fast food shortchanges your family's good eating habits.

It doesn't have to be this way. We all need a quick-fix mealtime solution every so often, but instead of turning to unhealthy takeout, stock your kitchen with enough basics to prepare, say, quick butter–Parmesan cheese pasta or refried black bean tacos.

By offering your child fresh, healthy, seasonal foods from her very first bites, you will reduce the number of junk-food battles. It is almost impossible in our society to completely avoid nutritionally bankrupt snacks. The best defense for overcoming the junk-food nation is to lay a sound nutritional foundation. When your child eats healthy food regularly, it gives her the wiggle room to indulge occasionally at a friend's house or a birthday party. Interestingly, I find that children who eat healthy meals on a regular basis are more likely to know their bodies limits.

I have seen families take many approaches to find a healthy food balance. Some eat healthy at home and indulge on the go; others like to make most of their food from scratch. Many other parents sneak healthy foods into their children's diets. You have to determine the right balance for your family. Remember, there is no one-size-fits-all approach.

> ## Sweetener Tip: Agave Nectar
>
> Agave nectar is a natural sweetener that even people with diabetes can eat. It has a low score on the glycemic index, which means it doesn't spike blood sugar levels or cause mood swings. You can pour agave on pancakes as a replacement for syrup, sweeten drinks with it, or use it in recipes as a substitute for sugar. Agave is so naturally sweet that you need only half of what you would with regular sugar to get the same sweet taste.
>
> Consider using other refined sugar alternatives, too, such as honey (discussed in Chapter 3), stevia, and molasses.

SWEET FOODS FILLED WITH LOVE (INSTEAD OF SUGAR)

Healthy Sweet Treats

Most American children eat far too much processed sugar. As a result, they never learn what naturally

Healthy On-the-Go Snacks

Stocking a snack cabinet or a refrigerator drawer with healthy snacks is one way to ensure that you always have healthy options on hand. Some favorites in my home include:

Apple slices with natural peanut butter or almond butter

Bagels with veggie cream spread

Baked sweet potato chips

Celery sticks with natural peanut butter or almond butter

Cereal bars

Fruit leather (100 percent fruit)

Fruit twist

Granola

Guacamole with veggies

Hummus with veggies or pita

Plain or cheese-flavored popcorn (after age 2)

Pretzels

Raisins, sweetened dried cranberries, or other dried fruit like mango and pineapple

Rice cakes

Seasonal fruits and berries

Seasonal veggies

String cheese

Veggie stick chips

Yogurt

---

sweetened treats taste like. Children who eat a lot of refined sugar often indulge in these foods in unhealthy ways, resulting in hyperactivity, mood swings, and poor nutrition. Sugar is tricky: It doesn't trigger the feeling of being full or satiated; instead, it leaves you wanting more and more. In contrast, when children eat healthy "growing" foods, they learn to recognize when their bodies are full.

Fortunately, there are ways to offer your children sweet treats without facing the side effects of too much sugar. Here are some ideas that parents will feel good about and kids will love. Take this excellent opportunity to reshape your own ideas about sweets and find the value in healthy alternatives that your whole family will enjoy.

nature's candy

Nature has its own candy, and it's called fruit! Eating sweet, ripe, in-season local fruit will help your children develop a taste for all types of fruits, including exotic varieties, and can help in your battle against refined sugar treats. Buy kiwifruit, mangoes, star fruit, lychee, pineapple, pomegranates, and other tropical fruits to encourage your children to broaden their horizons beyond apples, bananas, and oranges.

HELPFUL IDEAS

✓ Get a basket of red, juicy cherry tomatoes from your local farmers' market. I tell my kids those are nature's candy and they can feel free to eat as many as they want. It's nice not to have to limit their consumption or worry that they are eating too much sugar.

✓ My kids love to freeze grapes. They call them grape goodies. But beware: Grapes can pose a choking hazard for children until age 2, so be careful to cut whole grapes into small bites that you know your toddler can handle.

✓ For a refreshing treat, make smoothies with a juicer. Freeze the leftovers in ice-pop trays and eat the pops later in the day.

✓ Food can be fun when you prepare it in interesting shapes. Consider using cookie cutters on slices of fruits and vegetables.

DADDY WISDOM

"When visiting family, my daughter's uncle and aunt hosted a junk-food party for my daughter. While she enjoyed the soda, chips, and sugar, she also knew why her tummy hurt the next day. I feel she learned firsthand what I have been saying to her and now values eating healthy even more!"

Ian, daddy to Adrian, age 5

veronica's pumpkin poppers

These muffins are simple, delicious, and a nice treat for young and old. Pumpkins are full of brightly colored goodness—specifically, vitamins A and C. If your baby is just starting to chew, try crumbling the muffin so he can practice picking up pieces of food by himself.

MAKES 24

2 cups Pure Pumpkin Puree (page 43) or 1 (15 ounces) can unsweetened pumpkin

1 ripe banana, mashed

½ cup sweetened dried cranberries, chopped very small

2 eggs, well beaten

½ cup coconut milk

2 tablespoons agave nectar

1 tablespoon vanilla extract

2 cups whole wheat flour

2 teaspoons baking powder

½ teaspoon baking soda

1 teaspoon ground cinnamon

½ teaspoon freshly grated nutmeg

¼ teaspoon ground ginger

¼ teaspoon allspice

½ teaspoon sea salt

1 tablespoon ground pecans or walnuts

1 teaspoon ground flaxseed

1. Heat the oven to 375°F. Coat a mini muffin pan with organic cooking spray.

2. Combine the pumpkin puree, banana, cranberries, eggs, coconut milk, agave, and vanilla extract in a large mixing bowl.

3. Combine the flour, baking powder, baking soda, cinnamon, nutmeg, ginger, allspice, salt, nuts, and flaxseed in a separate bowl.

4. Fold the flour mixture into the pumpkin mixture ½ cup at a time.

5. Fill the prepared mini muffin pan with the batter. Bake for 20 to 25 minutes.

MAMA MANTRA

"I enjoy making sweets for my sweet baby, full of nutritional benefits and my love."

tia's sweet potato carob chip mini cakes

You don't have to feel guilty about giving your little ones a treat when you serve this tasty recipe. These mini cakes are packed with the nutrients of sweet potatoes and sweetened with agave nectar. Carob chips have a chocolatey taste without the caffeine. The cakes can be served as a fall seasonal treat—and you can replace the sweet potato with pumpkin, butternut squash, or even a sweet potato–kale mixture for added nutrition. I promise: These variations taste delicious! Although sweet potatoes can be found in your local markets all year, they are in season in November and December.

MAKES 12

1 cup Pure Sweet Potato Puree (page 38)

⅓ cup water

⅓ cup canola oil

2 tablespoons ground flaxseed

1 teaspoon vanilla extract

1⅔ cups whole wheat pastry flour

1 teaspoon baking powder

½ teaspoon baking soda

½ teaspoon kosher salt

½ teaspoon ground cinnamon

¼ teaspoon ground nutmeg

1 cup agave nectar

⅓ cup vegan carob chips

1. Preheat the oven to 350°F. Coat a nonstick muffin pan with cooking spray or insert paper liners.

2. Put the sweet potato puree, water, oil, flaxseed, and vanilla extract in a food processor. Blend well.

3. Whisk the flour, baking powder, baking soda, salt, cinnamon, and nutmeg in a large mixing bowl. Slowly add the agave. The nectar will be sticky, so fold it in thoroughly.

4. Add the sweet potato mixture to the flour mixture and then fold in the carob chips.

5. Spoon the batter into the prepared muffin pan, distributing evenly to make 12 muffins. Bake for 30 to 35 minutes, or until a toothpick inserted in the center of a muffin comes out clean. Cool on a wire rack. Serve warm.

Note: This recipe contains no refined sugar.

MAMA MANTRA

"Sweet potatoes are a powerhouse food for my sweet baby. It brings me great joy to offer healthy treats!"

sunshine's chocolate tofu pops

This recipe is made with organic raw dark chocolate, which is rich in antioxidants and cancer-fighting flavonoids. Processed chocolate contains refined sugars, but raw chocolate does not. If you want to stay away from chocolate altogether, this may not be the recipe for you. I believe that chocolate is fine in moderation, especially if you are using high-quality, organic, raw varieties.

MAKES 10

4 ounces silken tofu, drained

⅓ cup agave nectar

3 teaspoon ground almonds

⅓ cup organic raw dark unsweetened cocoa powder

½ cup coconut milk

1. Mix the tofu, agave, almonds, cocoa, and milk in a medium saucepan. Cook over medium heat until all ingredients melt together.

2. Pour the mixture into a blender or food processor and puree.

3. Pour into ice-pop molds. Freeze and enjoy.

   Note: This recipe contains no refined sugar.

Resources

BABY EXPERTS

Lauren Feder, MD
www.drfeder.com

Alan Greene, MD
www.drgreene.com

Jay Gordon, MD
www.drjaygordon.com/development/index.asp

Jim Sears, MD
www.askdrsears.com

Pump Station
http://www.pumpstation.com/pumpstation/

BABY-RELATED GROUPS & BLOGS

Amanda Blake Soule (my favorite Blog!)
http://www.soulemama.typepad.com/

Belly Sprout
www.bellysprout.com

City Mommy
www.citymommy.com

Green Moms
www.greenmoms.com

Healthy Child Healthy World
http://healthychild.org/

Holistic Moms Network
www.holisticmoms.org

Hot Moms Club
www.hotmomsclub.com

La Leche League
www.llli.org

Macaroni Kid
www.santamonica.macaronikid.com

Mama Source
www.mamasource.com

Mocha Moms
www.mochamoms.org

Moms Club
www.momsclub.org

Mothers & More
www.mothersandmore.org

CONSCIOUS COOKING

The Sacred Kitchen **by Robin Robertson**
www.amazon.com

Tassajara
www.sfzc.org/tassajara

EQUIPMENT

Beaba Babycook
www.beabausa.com

Coffee grinders
www.krupsonlinestore.com/product_list.
   asp?SKW=krugrind

Electric food mills
www.nextag.com/KidCo-F900-Electric-Baby-
   77733154/prices-html

Fresh baby food storage (Do not freeze glass)
www.amazon.com/Small-Storage-Serving-
   Container-Plastic/dp/B0018OULOM/ref=sr_1_5
   ?ie=UTF8&qid=1250393169&sr=8-5

"Green" cookware
www.green-pan.com

"Green" food mills
www.amazon.com/Green-Sprouts-Eco-friendly-
   Baby-Food/dp/B002F9MUL6

NATURAL CHILD-SIZE EQUIPMENT
(including high chairs, natural bowls, spoons, cups, and more)

For Small Hands
www.forsmallhands.com

Michael Olaf
www.michaelolaf.net

Nova Naturals
www.novanatural.com

Safe Sippy
www.kid-basix.com

Svan wooden high chair
www.svanusa.com/svanchair.cfm

GARDENING, FARMS, AND MARKETS

Composting made easy with Nature Mill
www.naturemill.com

MinifarmBox
www.minifarmbox.com/mfb/homebox.html

Paradise O
http://paradiseo.com

Pick-your-own farms
www.pickyourown.org

NATURAL BABY PRODUCTS

BPA-free ice-pop molds
www.amazon.com/Tovolo-Yellow-Groovy-Pop-
    Molds/dp/B000G32H3Y/ref=sr_1_1?ie=UTF8&s
    =home-garden&qid=1250370054&sr=1-1

Chapter One Organics
http://chapteroneorganics.com/

Dress Me Up
www.dressmeup.com

Earth Mama Angel Baby
http://www.earthmamaangelbaby.com/index.php

Ergo Baby Carrier
http://www.ergobabycarrier.com/

Gdiapers
http://www.gdiapers.com/

Giggle
http://www.giggle.com

Greencradle
http://www.greencradle.com

Hip Mountain Mama
http://www.hipmountainmama.com/

Innovative Baby
www.innovative-baby.com

Kate Quinn Organics
www.katequinnorganics.com

Kelly's Closet
http://www.kellyscloset.com/crm.asp?action=add

Klean Kanteen
www.kleankanteen.com/

Mighty Nest
http://www.mightynest.com

Moby Wrap
http://www.mobywrap.com/

Nature's Baby
http://www.naturesbabyproducts.com

Rebe
www.myrebe.com

Tiny Revolutionary
http://www.tinyrevolutionary.com

Uppa Baby
http://www.uppababy.com

Zooni
http://www.zooniwear.com

EXTRAS

Alexandra Du Furio Photography
www.defuriophotography.com

Bag Lady Promotions
www.bagladypromotions.com

BASH Eco-Events
http://www.bashecoevents.com/

EcoStiletto
http://www.ecostiletto.com/

Fresh Mommy Food Delivery
www.freshology.com/

Gina Sabatella Photography
www.sabatellafoto.com

Highland Hall Waldorf School
www.highlandhall.org

LOVE food Delivery
http://lovedelivery.com/main.html

My Kids Art on Canvas
www.MyKidsArtOnCanvas.com

24–7
www.damarisradut.com

Endnotes

CHAPTER 1

1. Lauren Feder, MD, *Natural Baby and Childcare: Practical Medical Advice and Holistic Wisdom for Raising Healthy Children* (New York: Healthy Living Books, 2006), 196–197.

2. Environment California, *Toxic Baby Bottles,* http://www.environmentcalifornia.org/reports/environmental-health/environmental-health-reports/toxic-baby-bottles.

3. Tina [no last name given], "Why Cow's Milk Isn't Really Good for You, and Why Soy Milk Isn't Either," *Healthy Dialogues,* February 27, 2009, http://healthydialogues.blogspot.com/2009/02/hy-cows-milk-isnt-really-good-for-you.html.

4. Linda Folden Palmer, DC, "The Dangers of Cow's Milk," http://www.naturalchild.org/guest/linda_folden_palmer.html.

CHAPTER 2

1. Dale and Melissa Kent, *Tassajara Dinner and Desserts* (Gibbs Smith, 2009)

CHAPTER 3

1. Jay Gordon, MD, "Infant Cereal and Juice," http://www.drjaygordon.com/development/faqs/faq038.asp.

2. American Academy of Pediatrics Committee on Nutrition, *The Use and Misuse of Fruit Juice in Pediatrics,* http://aappolicy.aappublications.org/cgi/reprint/pediatrics;107/5/1210.

3. Feder, *Natural Baby and Childcare,* 242

4. Ibid., 241

5. Ibid., 230–231

6. John Soy Henkel, "Health Claims for Soy Protein, Questions about Other Components," *FDA Consumer,* May 2000; also available at http://www.foodconsumer.org/777/8/Eating_soy_protein_benefits_the_heart_shtml.

7. Feder, *Natural Baby and Childcare,* 245–246

8. Mayo Clinc staff, "Organic Foods: Are They Safer? More Nutritious?" http://www.mayoclinic.com/health/organic-food/NU00255.

9. Madeline Miller, "There's No Such Thing as 'USDA Organic' Fish," http://growersandgrocers.net/2006/12/05/theres-no-such-thing-as-usda-organic-fish/.

10. Feder, *Natural Baby and Childcare.*

11. Wholesomebabyfood.com, "Myths and Facts about Nitrates and Homemade Baby Food," http://www.wholesomebabyfood.com/nitratearticle.htm.

12. L. Fenicia, A. M. Ferrini, P. Aureli, and M. Pocecco, "A Case of Infant Botulism Associated with Honey Feeding in Italy," *European Journal of Epidemiology* 9 (no. 6), November 1993, 671–73.

CHAPTER 4

1. James A. Joseph, Daniel A. Nadeau, and Anne Underwood, *The Color Code* (New York: Philip Leaf Group, 2002), xv.

2. David Heber, *What Color Is Your Diet?* (New York: Regan Books, 2001), also available at http://www.yale.edu/ynhti/curriculum/units/2007/5/07.05.05.x.html.

CHAPTER 5

1. Elizabeth Pivonka, PhD, RD, "The Health Benefits of Avacados [*sic*]," http://www.doityourself.com/stry/avacados.

2. Peggy Trowbridge Filippone, "Mango History," http://homecooking.about.com/od/foodhistory/a/mangohistory.htm.

3. George Mateljan Foundation for the World's Healthiest Foods, "Green Beans," http://www.whfoods.com/genpage.php?tname=foodspice&dbid=134.

4. George Mateljan Foundation for the World's Healthiest Foods, "Asparagus," http://www.whfoods.com/genpage.php?tname=foodspice&dbid=12.

5. BellyBytes.com, "Butternut and Acorn Squash," http://www.bellybytes.com/food/squash.html.

CHAPTER 7

1. Benjamin Spock, MD, *Dr. Spock's Baby and Child Care,* 7th ed. (New York, Dutton Adult, 1998), http://www.nytimes.com/1998/06/30/science/personal-health-feeding-children-off-the-spock-menu.html

2. Jay Gordon, MD, *Good Food Today, Great Kids Tomorrow: 50 Things You Can Do for Healthy, Happy Children* (Michael Wiese Film Productions, September 1994), also available at http://www.yale.edu/ynhti/curriculum/units/2007/5/07.05.05.x.html.

3. Alan Greene, MD, "Healthy Eating, Part II: What Foods Do Children Need? What Foods Should Be Avoided?" http://www.drgreene.com/21_191.html.

4. William Sears, MD, *The Family Nutrition Book: Everything You Need to Know about Feeding Your Children—From Birth through Adolescence* (Boston: Little, Brown, 1999), http://www.parenting.com/article/Toddler/Recipes—Nutrition-For-Children/Ask-Dr-Sears-Raising-a-Vegetarian-Child

5. *Vegetarianism: An Ecological Perspective* (Loma Linda, CA: Andrews University, 1994).

6. Carol [no last name given], "What Is Gluten and What Damage Does It Do?" http://www.the-gluten-free-chef.com/what-is-gluten.html.

7. Kathy Summers, "Getting Healthy Together," *Natural Health,* July/August 2008, http://www.kathysummers.com/natural_health/

CHAPTER 10

1. Kellymom.com, "Nutrition for Nursing Toddlers," http://www.kellymom.com/nutrition/solids/toddler-foods.html.

Acknowledgments

FROM ANNI

To my dear mom who has always, and in all ways, supported my every endeavor. I love you, Mom.

To my mother-in-law and father-in-law, Bonnie and Dan Walter, for your love and kindness and endless support.

To my nieces and nephews Austin, Cameron, Finn, Kael, Alex, and Gracie, whom I adore to no end.

To Jenn for your courage to follow your heart.

To Jessie and Kevin for your support.

To Meredith, my agent, for your endless advocating and love of all my ideas.

To Shanté Lanay for your hard work on the book and all those long nights of editing.

To my best friend, Tanya McAllister, for your love, support, happy energy, and ability to always make me laugh. To you and Teene for your sweetness and love of our children.

To Piper for your loving friendship.

To Brandie and Carmine who helped us realize the original vision, and who are dear friends.

To Pedro, Carlos, and Manuel for making Bohemian Baby have heart and soul.

To Michelle and David for being our first Bo Baby customers and for your help with the Web site.

To my husband, Tim, whom I love more than all the "I love you's" ever said! Your spiritual quest motivates me and gives me the courage to keep moving every day. Thank you, sweetheart.

To Zoë, whom I love more than all words ever written. Your humor and appreciation of food is inspiring. Your creativity is astonishing, and I can't wait to see what you do with your life.

To Lotus Sunshine, whom I love more than all the stars in the sky. You are the brightest light in every room, and your pure, sweet energy inspires me in every moment.

To my dear little Bodhi, whom I love more than all the cookies ever eaten. You are pure joy. I love watching you dance and run around, and there is nothing better than a big hug from you.

To my newest addition growing inside: We are all excited to meet you, and we can't wait to play with you and love you.

FROM SHANTÉ

I have been blessed with a wonderful circle of support for which I am eternally grateful. Mackenzie, my beautiful daughter, mama loves you more than the ocean is wide.

Aziza, Anni, Meredith, Lolita, Brandon, Arielle, Camille, Lorenzo, Elizabeth and my soul sister Windy: My hope is that we continue growing closer as friends. Doreen Arriaga, "Editorial Goddess," and Arianna McClain, "Child Nutrition Goddess": This project would never have blossomed without your insights and friendship. While my friendships are incomparable, my life would be colorless without the love and circle of support from my amazing *ohana*! THANK GOD FOR MY FAMILY! Mom, Dad, RJ, Rian, Grandma Carolyn, Grandpa Verne, Uncle Darryl, Aunt Valerie, Uncle Chace, Cy, Leah, Morgan, TJ, Nonnie and the entire family up north: I cherish you all.

FROM BOTH OF US

To Gena and Pam, the "Rodale Goddesses," for seeing this vision and believing in *Organically Raised* from the beginning and for support, patience, and enthusiasm.

To Gina Sabatella for your amazing photography, vision, and endless patience.

Huge thanks to all of you who helped with our photo shoots: To Highland Hall Waldorf School for the use of the beautiful campus. To Patti Haines for the use of your lovely home. To Kate Quinn Organics for lending your gorgeous organic clothes. To Rebe for the use of your innovative and sweet clothes. To Erin and Nick Cloak at Innovative Baby for being my dear friends and endless supporters and for the use of your darling clothes. To Elizabeth Shahbazi for your contribution of lovely flowers.

To all the babies who played with us, ate our food, and let us take your pictures for the book: We are so grateful to you and your parents.

Index

Vinaigrette
    Shanté's Seared Mahi Mahi
        Lettuce Cups with Shaved
        Romano, Walnuts, and
        Creamy Vinaigrette
        Dressing, 126
Vitamin A, sources of, 23
Vitamin C, sources of, 23
Vitamin D, 93–94

W

Waffles
    Alex's All-American Whole
        Wheat Apple-Pumpkin
        Waffles with Cinnamon
        Agave Syrup, 103
Walnuts
    Lorrin's Basil-Walnut Pesto
        Quesadilla, 119
    Shanté's Seared Mahi Mahi
        Lettuce Cups with Shaved
        Romano, Walnuts, and

    Creamy Vinaigrette
        Dressing, 126
Water, flavorings for, 15, _15_
Watermelon
    Noni's Cold Watermelon Soup,
        174, **175**
Web sites
    on food preparation equipment,
        9
    listing high and low sprayed
        produce, xvi
    on locally grown foods, xvii
    on natural parenting tips, ix
Wheat, protein in, 17
Wheat germ, as mix-in, _11_, **58**, 59
Whole grains. _See_ Grains

Y

Yams, garnet. _See_ Sweet potatoes
Yellow squash
    Baby Tara's "Winter Goodness"
        Yellow Squash, Carrot,

        Apple, and Broccoli Blend
        (winter), 80
    nutrients in, _43_
    Pure Yellow Squash Puree
        (summer), 43
Yogurt combinations
    Baby Apple's Apple and
        Cranberry Yogurt (winter),
        87
    Baby Bonnie's Banana-Berry
        Yogurt (spring), 87
    Baby Charlie's Apple and Mango
        Yogurt (fall), 87, **87**
    Baby Joy's Peach-Raspberry-
        Açai Yogurt (summer), 88

Z

Zucchini
    Ginger's Asian Stir-Fry, 142
    nutrients in, _44_
    Pure Zucchini Squash Puree
        (summer), 44